W9-BHS-629

PRAISE FOR

Good-Bye High School, Hello World

This book is filled with everything I want to tell my daughter as she prepares for young adulthood. Bruce and Stan understand and relate to this age group in a wonderful way. This book is the new Burns family graduation gift!

JIM BURNS, PH.D.
PRESIDENT, HOMEWORD

Bruce and Stan draw from real experience to give us a must-read book for those graduating from high school (or recently graduated) and their parents.

CLYDE COOK
PRESIDENT, BIOLA UNIVERSITY, LA MIRADA, CALIFORNIA

Wow! This is a must-have manual for making the zillion and one transitions from high school to real life. From dorms to dating, careers to character, parents to professors, Bruce and Stan have got you covered.

ANDREA STEPHENS
AUTHOR, *GIRLFRIEND, YOU ARE A B.A.B.E.!*

Good-Bye High School, Hello World is like a trusted, experienced friend pulling you aside and giving you the real scoop on one of the scariest and most exciting times in your life. This book is a must-have for any college student—even more important than a microwave and a minifridge!

TIM WALKER

EDITOR, *YOUTHWALK* MAGAZINE

Bruce and Stan are marvelously connected with post-high school students, keenly perceptive about what faces them, and amazingly gifted in communicating with them about integrating faith and life. This is a wonderful resource for young men and women. My only regret is that it wasn't available when I was in my late teens!

DAVID K. WINTER

CHANCELLOR, WESTMONT COLLEGE, SANTA BARBARA, CALIFORNIA

Goodbye High School, Hello World

Bruce Bickel
& Stan Jantz

Lamppost Library & Resource Center
Christ United Methodist Church
4488 Poplar Avenue
Memphis, Tennessee 38117

Regal

From Gospel Light
Ventura, California, U.S.A.

Regal

PUBLISHED BY REGAL BOOKS
FROM GOSPEL LIGHT
VENTURA, CALIFORNIA, U.S.A.
PRINTED IN THE U.S.A.

Regal Books is a ministry of Gospel Light, a Christian
publisher dedicated to serving the local church. We believe God's vision
for Gospel Light is to provide church leaders with biblical, user-friendly
materials that will help them evangelize, disciple and minister to
children, youth and families.

It is our prayer that this Regal book will help you discover
biblical truth for your own life and help you meet the needs
of others. May God richly bless you.

*For a free catalog of resources from Regal Books/Gospel Light,
please call your Christian supplier or contact us at* 1-800-4-GOSPEL
or www.regalbooks.com.

Rights for publishing this book in other languages are contracted by
Gospel Light Worldwide, the international nonprofit ministry of Gospel
Light. Gospel Light Worldwide also provides publishing and technical
assistance to international publishers dedicated to producing Sunday School
and Vacation Bible School curricula and books in the languages of the
world. For additional information, visit www.gospellightworldwide.org;
write to Gospel Light Worldwide, P.O. Box 3875, Ventura, CA 93006; or
send an e-mail to info@gospellightworldwide.org.

All Scripture quotations are taken from the *Holy Bible, New Living Translation*, copyright © 1996. Used by permission of Tyndale House Publishers, Inc., Wheaton, Illinois 60189. All rights reserved.

Originally published as *Real Life Begins After High School* by Servant Publications in 2000.
Updated and revised edition published by Regal in 2005.

© 2000 Bruce Bickel and Stan Jantz
All rights reserved.

Library of Congress Cataloging-in-Publication Data

Bickel, Bruce, 1952-
  [Real life begins after high school]
  Good-bye high school, hello world / Bruce Bickel and Stan Jantz.
      p. cm.
  Originally published: Real life begins after high school. Ann Arbor, Mich.: Vine Books, c2000.
  Includes bibliographical references.
  ISBN 0-8307-3728-6 (hardcover) — ISBN 0-8307-3733-2 (trade pbk.)
  1. Young adults—Religious life. 2. High school graduates—Religious life.
3. Young adults—Conduct of life. 4. High school graduates—Conduct of life. 5. Christian life. I. Jantz, Stan, 1952- II. Title.

BV4528.2.B535 2005
248.8'3—dc22   2004030633

1 2 3 4 5 6 7 8 9 10 / 11 10 09 08 07 06 05

Contents

A Note from the Authors...8

Introduction...10

Chapter 1..15
Custom Design Yourself
Who Do You Want to Be?

Chapter 2..32
College
Growing Smarter by Degrees

Chapter 3..48
Forwarding Address
Growing Up Usually Means Moving Out

Chapter 4..64
Your Character
It's Who You Really Are

Chapter 5..81
Friends
Choose or Lose

Chapter 6..97
More Than Friends
Dating and Beyond

Contents

Chapter 7..112
Money Matters
Your Fiscal Fitness Program

Chapter 8..128
Healthy Choices
Preparing Your Body to Last a Lifetime

Chapter 9..143
Family Ties
Out of Sight, but Not Forgotten

Chapter 10..157
Jobs and Careers
So What Are You Going to Do?

Chapter 11..173
God and Your Worldview
Can You See Forever?

Chapter 12..186
Those Things You Do
What God Wants for You

Endnotes..201

Bibliography...202

A Note from the Authors

This book is specifically and exclusively written to those students who have recently graduated from high school (or are about to). If that's not you, then put this book down. If it is you, then keep reading.

What you'll find in this book comes a little bit from us, Bruce and Stan, and a lot from the college-aged guys and gals whom we have known over the past few years. We even contacted many of them during the writing of this book and asked for some specific advice and "words of wisdom." You'll find their quotes sprinkled throughout the following pages.

But there is more to this book than just practical advice and information. The most important part of our lives is our faith in God. That spiritual dimension brings balance, hope and confidence to all other aspects and details of our lives. We can't honestly talk about your future without including God in the discussion. Actually, it is amazing to realize that God has a specific plan for you:

> "For I know the plans I have
> for you," says the LORD.
> "They are plans for good and not for disaster,
> to give you a future and a hope" (Jeremiah 29:11).

If you are serious about making plans for the next few years, you ought to at least consider what God says about your future.

We are genuinely excited for you because we know that the next several years in your life are going to be a great adventure. You'll experience a combination of freedom, responsibility, learning and recreation that won't be matched at any other stage in your life. With our help, maybe, just maybe, you can do it without ending up in debt, in the hospital or in jail.

Bruce Bickel
Stan Jantz

Introduction

Because you are reading this book, you are probably a recent high school graduate or at least counting the days that you have left.

For your first 17 years or so, your parents and other adults dictated the circumstances of your life. In a big way, they decide where you would live, what you would do and with whom you would do it. Oh, sure, you had your own personally selected group of friends, and you had freedom of choice to a limited degree. But let's be honest: It wasn't really your choice to spend the Fourth of July weekend at Great Aunt Marion's house while she recovered from her bunionectomy.

By your eighteenth birthday and high school graduation, however, you enter an awkward transitional stage. We don't mean awkward in the sense of being uncoordinated and clumsy. (That happened in middle school. You have, no doubt, outgrown that stage and now move with grace and dignity—or at least without stumbling over the paint lines in the parking lot.) We mean awkward in a bizarre sense:

- The law says you are an adult, but your parents say you aren't.
- You are old enough to join the military and

fire antiaircraft missiles, but your parents don't want you playing paintball because you might get hurt.

· Your parents tell you to assume more responsibility for yourself, but they feel compelled to remind you to carry tissues when you have a cold.

Exactly What You Didn't Know You Needed

What you could use at this awkward stage of your life is exactly what you don't think you need: advice. We're not talking about the advice your parents gave you during those lectures you didn't listen to. We're assuming you already know these things:

· If everybody jumps off a cliff, you shouldn't do it.

· Don't drive without a seat belt; don't run with scissors; and don't step outside the house in just your underwear.

· Smoking cigarettes is a disgusting habit (even if it qualifies you to be a plaintiff in a multi-million-dollar lawsuit against the tobacco companies).

We're talking about advice on the aspects of life that you haven't experienced yet.

> **You know a lot about what you know. But you don't know much about what you don't know.**

Your lack of knowledge doesn't mean you can't survive on your own; it just means you need to learn a little bit more about what you don't know.

When your parents tell you these things, (a) you won't listen, or (b) they will be upset (or at least disappointed) if you don't follow their "suggestions." But not us. We don't know you, and we haven't shelled out big bucks for 18 years to keep you in high-fashion footwear and braces. So our feelings won't be hurt if you question our wisdom or scoff at our advice. But just in case you're worried that we might get a little parental on you, here's what we promise:

- *We'll be objective with you.* We've got no ulterior motives. Unlike some parents, we aren't looking to you to support us in our old age. So we don't have any particular career path already picked out for you. We don't care if your ideal job is to publish newspapers or to deliver them. We'll tell you the good and the bad and the pros and the cons without trying to influence you. We'll give you the facts as we see them, and then you can make up your own mind.

- *We won't lecture you.* There is no finger wagging in this book. Our eyes won't bulge and our faces won't turn red as we tell you this stuff. We'll stay calm and serene. We have opinions, and we'll let you know them. But we know that you have opinions, too. Unfortunately, we can't hear your opinions, but we respect them anyway. After all, we know it is your life we are talking about, and we'll assume that you aren't trying to mess it up on purpose. So we can't say that our opinions on everything are definitely right for you and that yours are wrong. Consider what we have to say as "friendly suggestions." That's how we intend it. You can take it or leave it.

- *We'll be interactive with you.* We are anxious to hear your feedback. What did you find useful in the book? What could be tossed? Is there something with which you strongly agree or disagree in this book? Do you have insights and experiences of your own that other people could learn from? Well, let us know. We promise that we'll personally respond to you. There are several ways you can contact us.

E-mail: info@christianity101online.com
Web site: www.christianity101online.com
Snailmail: Bruce and Stan
P.O. Box 25997
Fresno, CA 93729-5565

Let us know how things are going for you at any point in the process.

Moving On

Well, you've been reading this introduction long enough. It's time to jump into the book and start thinking about your future. You can start right at chapter 1 and go straight through, or you can skip around. It doesn't matter to us. You decide for yourself. You're getting ready for real life, so you better start making decisions on your own (although we'll admit that most decisions in your life will be much more difficult than deciding which chapter to read next).

Custom Design Yourself

Who Do You Want to Be?

*Regardless of what some say, high school
is not the best time of your life.
It only gets better. And you should get better with it.*

LINDSEY B., AGE 21

Your graduation from high school has much more significance than the decorative diploma that you get for completing your senior year. The diploma is a symbol that you completed the work, but graduation itself marks a new beginning in your life. Once you cross the stage after shaking hands with your principal (and some faceless school board member who mispronounced your name), you will walk through a hole in the time-space continuum, and your life will never be the same.

Leaving Your Past Behind

Just when you've mastered the high school thing, you are ripped out of the comfort zone of the old campus, the old teachers (and for some of them, we do mean *old*) and the friends you have had since kindergarten. You're suddenly thrown into the abyss of the unknown: life *after* high school.

Before the panic sets in and you sign up for a second senior year, let us offer another perspective. Sure, it is scary, and we won't deny that initially your life will not be as certain as the day-in, day-out high school routine, but think about the benefits of moving on with your life and leaving all of that high school baggage behind.

This is your chance to ditch the stereotypes you have carried around since middle school. No one will care about who you used to be or what you used to do. Their opinion will be based on your present performance and personality; their judgment of you will have nothing to do with the reputation you got in the seventh grade. (That will be a refreshing change for you.)

Your new friends will never suspect that you were once an ugly duckling. They won't know that your appearance was technically augmented and visually enhanced by braces and a nose job.

That embarrassing nickname will be gone forever. Nobody will be calling you "little Patti underpants" or "Tyler the Crier" based on some humiliating episode that you suffered in elementary school.

Best of all, you can create a whole new you. The slate is clean. All of the previously established notions of who you are will suddenly vanish. You can create a whole new you. Maybe an entire overhaul isn't necessary; perhaps just a little fine-tuning will be all it takes. Whether you want to scrap everything and start all over, or just make a few minor adjustments, now is your perfect opportunity to do it.

Where Do You Want to Go?

When you were just a little tyke, your mother probably laid out your clothes for you each morning. (In the last few years, that hasn't been necessary, because your clothes were probably already laid out—all over the floor.) And the rest of your life was pretty much laid out for you, too. In high school, you had a few electives, but you had no choice about English, math,

If you don't care where you are going, then it doesn't matter how you get there.

science and P.E. But now you are free from such rigid structure. Your future is not laid out for you. It is up to you to decide where you want to go.

What if you decide to embark on your journey into the future without a plan? Well, we sure wouldn't recommend it, but it will take some pressure off you—for now. Planning becomes irrelevant if you have no destination in mind.

In fact, you might be tempted to approach your future with a cavalier, carefree attitude. After all, your past few years have been pretty intense (with school, dating, working, parents, sports and more). Maybe you feel like you deserve a rest.

Failing to Plan=Planning to Fail

As appealing as that may seem, failure to plan at this point in your life will probably make your life harder, not easier. Now is the best time to gain the education and experience that you'll need for certain jobs and careers. Think about it.

- *The older you are, the more complicated life will become.* It will be tough to go back to college when you are 34 years old, with a spouse and two toddlers. (And it is no fun living in a college dorm if you have to miss the water balloon fights because you are changing your kid's diapers.)
- *You won't always be able to live this cheaply.* Now you can probably survive quite nicely on a minimum wage job, but that 1993 Ford Escort that you are driving has a limited life expectancy. Sooner or later you'll be wishing for a higher paying job.
- *Some doors will close if you wait too long to walk through them.* It's too late to decide to be an astronaut, for example, if you are already collecting Social Security.
- *There's no time like the present to plan for your future.* Fifteen years from now, you don't want

to be standing on the median at a busy inter-section, asking for donations as the cars drive by, with a message scribbled on a piece of cardboard that reads, "I didn't plan to fail; I just failed to plan."

Look Past Tomorrow

Your crystal ball is probably a little murky, but take a good look into your future. We don't mean the future of next week or even next year. Look harder. What do you see in your future 5 years from now?

> **Most people spend more time planning a two-week vacation than they spend planning for the rest of their life.**

How about 15 years from now? What do you see yourself doing? What kind of job do you have? Where are you living? What are you doing for fun with your friends? Are you involved with your church? Are you helping with any community charitable organizations? What is your family situation? How are you spending your money?

We know these are tough questions to answer when the ink on your high school diploma is still wet. But a little long-range life planning shouldn't seem too strange.

Are You Nearsighted or Farsighted?

When it comes to seeing the future, many people suffer from a vision problem. Here are two of the most common:

- *Nearsighted.* The person with a nearsighted vision of the future only sees what is in the world immediately around them. The jobs they see in the future are the same jobs that their parents have. Their view of the future is limited to the geographic region in which they have lived. Their future is restricted by what they can see in their present experience.
- *Farsighted.* With a far-sighted view of the future, you can see beyond your own experience. Maybe you have grown up in a large metropolitan center, but you can see the possibility of living in a small rural community. Maybe your grandfather was a physician, and your father

The best person for the job is the one who works hard enough to do the job best.

was a physician, and you always thought you'd be a physician, too, because that is all that you knew. But if you have a farsighted vision of the future, perhaps you can see yourself owning and operating a bed-and-breakfast inn near Vail, Colorado (using the parlor for appendectomy surgeries during the off-season).

Being far-sighted about your future doesn't mean you have to reject what is familiar to you. It just means that you are open to consider other options than what you have already experienced.

A Change in Priorities

Until now, your personal priorities didn't matter very much because you were living in a pattern that was determined for you by someone else. Lots of people were anxious to set the parameters of your life: your parents, your teachers and high school administrators, your coaches or employers, even your friends. As you begin life on your own, however, you will find that you have much more freedom to determine for yourself what is important *to you*.

So, what *is* important to you? Now is the time when you get to decide for yourself. Why is this important? We're glad you asked. Lots of things and people are going to be competing for your time: new friends, your roommates, your college classes and your job. Other important parts of your life might get lost in the shuffle: your relationship with God, your parents, your siblings and your old friends. You need to determine now what is important so that you can make sure that important aspects of your life don't get overlooked.

Reality Check

Just for fun, take a moment to jot down six priorities of your life. This isn't like a pop quiz; it won't be graded. We just want you to try a little experiment. If you can, arrange them in the order of importance to you. To make it easier, we'll even give you a place to write them. Go ahead, we'll wait.

The priorities of my life include

1. _____
2. _____
3. _____
4. _____
5. _____
6. _____

Now, check to see if those priorities are reflected in your life. Here's an easy way to verify whether you are living your life according to your priorities. Ask yourself these two questions:

- *How am I spending my time?* What you consider to be important to you probably isn't a priority unless you are spending time on it. You know this from personal experience. If someone says that you are her best friend, but she doesn't spend any time with you, you know that you aren't much of a priority in her life. Similarly, you might think that your relationship with God has a priority in your life, but that is doubtful if your only prayers are uttered during finals week. Where you spend your time is a good indicator of your priorities.

- *How am I spending my money?* You can learn a lot about yourself by tracking how you spend your money. Sure, most of the entries show money spent on yourself, and there is nothing wrong with that. Hey, you've got to eat, and you can't walk around naked. But have you given any money to charity or ministries? Does your bank statement show that you are thinking of others or just yourself? You've got a big inconsistency in your life if you say that education is a priority but your check card receipts show that you are at the movies three times a week.

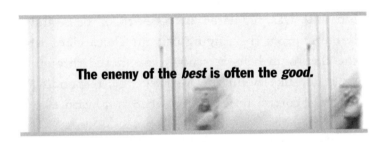

The enemy of the *best* is often the *good*.

The way that you spend your time, energy, money and resources is the best way to discover your priorities. If you don't like what that tells you, then start doing the things that you believe should have more importance in your life. Take the time to determine your priorities so that you will know what is important to you. Once you have determined what is important, you can ignore the trivial things without feeling guilty.

Where Does It Go?

Here's a riddle for you:

You have the same amount as everybody else, But you never have enough, and you always want more. What is it?

Don't waste too much *time* pondering this question, because *time* is exactly what you don't have enough of. As a high school student, your daily schedule was regulated by a series of bells and buzzers. From the ringing of your alarm clock to the classroom bells at school, you moved through your day like Bobo the Monkey Boy, responding with the correct reflex action when you heard each noise.

Your life after high school will be a lot quieter. There aren't as many bells. That's the good news. The bad news is that it will be more difficult for you to stay on schedule. You won't have the routine of high school. You'll have much more freedom, and it will be your own responsibility to make sure everything gets handled on time. There is so much that you will want to do. You will have to learn how to distinguish the important things from the unimportant ones.

The challenge in time management is not deciding between the *important* and the *trivial*. Instead, you will frequently be required to choose between activities that are equally good or equally important. If you have a good grasp on your priorities, then you'll be better equipped to distinguish between what is *good* and what is *best*.

Just Say No

If you are a person who is usually overcommitted, you have a time management problem. It probably won't go away by itself. People will keep asking you to do things because (1) you get things done and (2) you always say yes when you are asked to do something. Realize that the people who make requests of you aren't sensitive to whether you are under so much stress that your hair is falling out and your gastric juices could burn through steel. They are primarily interested in getting the job done, and they are glad that you are willing to do it. For your own sanity, learn to say no. You are too young to be bald and have an ulcer.

The Art of Goal Setting

Are you intimidated by the thought of assuming greater responsibility for your life? Does it seem overwhelming? Well, don't get discouraged. There are some definite steps you can take to get a handle on managing your life.

Step 1: Dissect Yourself

Put the scalpel away. This is about dividing your life into different dimensions or roles. Most people live their lives in seven basic categories:

> *Spiritual*—your relationship with God
> *Physical*—your health and recreation
> *Mental*—your intellectual growth
> *Financial*—how you spend and save your money
> *Social*—your relationships and activities with friends
> *Occupational*—what you do to earn a living
> *Familial* (it sounds awkward, but it's a word)—your relationships with your family members.

You are probably having mixed success in the different dimensions of your life. In some areas you may be doing fine; maybe others could use a little help.

Take God's Word for It

If you are interested in knowing what God has to say about the different dimensions of your life, check out these passages:

Spiritual—Jeremiah 17:5-8   **Social**—Proverbs 17:7

Physical—Psalm 139:14   **Occupational**—Proverbs 12:14

Mental—Proverbs 10:14   **Familial**—Ephesians 5:21—6:4

Financial—Proverbs 3:9

Step 2: Determine Your Objectives

In each of the seven dimensions, determine an *objective* for improvement. Even in the strong areas of your life, there is room for improvement. For example, you may want to set a spiritual objective to get to know God better.

Step 3: Set a Goal to Reach Each Objective

Once you have determined your noble objectives, you need to set a *goal* that directs your actions toward achieving those objectives. Objectives are usually general in nature, but goals are specific. For example, to reach your spiritual objective of getting to know God better, you might set a goal to read through the Bible in a year.

> **Surveys show that only 10 percent of the population have goals, and only 3 percent have put their goals in writing.**

After you have set your goals, put them in writing and review them regularly. Don't forget to reward yourself when you reach your goal.

You Are a Lifelong Project

You are an ever-changing, evolving creature. We aren't talking about Darwin's theory that a banana slug turns into a moose after a few generations. We're talking about your spiritual, emotional and intellectual growth as a person. Deciding who you are and the kind of person you want to become isn't a task confined to the age range of 18 to 21 years. It is a lifelong process, but right after high school is a great time to get started.

Moving On

We wanted to devote the first chapter in this book to discussing the kind of person you are and the kind of person you want to become. Before you go too far with your life after high school, you need to come to grips with your personal priorities and values. Whatever you believe, you will find people who will have contrary opinions and opposing views.

You will find the greatest conglomeration of philosophies, attitudes and beliefs on the college campus. There are many people there who will be tolerant and accepting of who you are and what you believe. Others, however, will have nothing but hostility for viewpoints other than their own. Interaction with people who agree with you and confrontation with those who don't will be important parts of your life experience. Whether they happen in the dormitory, in the dining commons, on the quad or in class, your discussions about the meaning of life will stimulate and challenge you.

But there is a lot more to college than lofty philosophizing, and in the next chapter we'll give you an overview of what you can expect.

Lamppost Library & Resource Center
Christ United Methodist Church
4488 Poplar Avenue
Memphis, Tennessee 38117

College

Growing Smarter by Degrees

Learn how to study.

JOHN K., AGE 22

College is an amazing thing. No other earthly institution you will encounter in your lifetime will have as much potential to affect, influence, mold, direct, discourage, energize, prepare, poop out, enlighten, frustrate and change you—all in the space of a few years.

What Is College Anyway?

On the one hand, college is very *tangible*, because it's a place. When you tell people, "I attend Westmont College" or "I'm going to Iowa State," they immediately think of a campus with buildings and trees and dormitories (even if they don't know where Westmont or Iowa actually is).

The oldest institution in the United States is Harvard University, which was founded in 1636, only 16 years after the Pilgrims landed at Plymouth Rock.

On the other hand, college is *intangible*, because in many ways it's a state of mind. When you tell people, "I'm a college student," they probably think of all the stuff you are learning. (They also wonder how much you're goofing off, but they won't mention this because they once went to college, too.)

What If College Isn't for You?

College isn't for everyone, although the excuse "I don't like to study" isn't a good reason to avoid college. There are legitimate reasons why college may not be right for you—at least for right now:

- You started a high-tech company in your room while you were in high school, and you've just been bought out by Microsoft.
- You've been working in your dad's construction business since you were old enough to tote a brick, and you know that is what you want to do for your future.
- You want to spend a year serving God on a short-term missions trip.
- You figure the growth occupation of the future will be tattoo removals, and you want to learn the skill now in order to be ready for all those Gen-Xers when their skin starts to sag.

You may have some very good reasons for not continuing your education past high school (or at least not going to college right away). But don't discount the college experience too quickly. Even those who decide not to pursue a bachelor's degree may want to take a few courses or even earn an associate's degree to give them special skills for whatever they want to do, from running a business to becoming a better stay-at-home parent. So if you know for sure that college isn't for you, then skip the rest of this chapter. But if college is a certainty or even a possibility, keep reading.

What Are Your College Options?

For the last 18 years or so, pretty much everything you've done has been planned for you ahead of time: the food you ate, the clothes you wore, where you went to church, where you went to school, what classes you took and what you learned. Oh, you may think you've had options, but they've been pretty limited. Well, that's about to change. You're an adult now (or you're almost there), and the world of options is about to open up to you in a big way. Let's look at some of the big considerations when choosing a college.

Staying Home or Going Away

Whether to attend college in your hometown or to go out of town is a major decision requiring much thought, a thorough investigation and many discussions with your family. Several factors affect this decision, not the least of which is financial. In addition, you need to do an honest self-evaluation to determine if you are ready to leave home (of course, as long as you can bring dirty laundry home on weekends, you haven't *really* left).

Many students prefer the option of attending a junior or community college in their hometown for the first couple of years and then transferring to a four-year college or university for the rest of their education. This can be an efficient and cost-effective means of getting through college. Consequently, many parents prefer this option (unless they are anxious for you to go away so that they can remodel your room with a spa and sauna).

Private or Public
Cost is probably the biggest factor in whether to choose a private or a public college. Every state has a college and university system that benefits resident students. The cost of a private college education seems almost prohibitive to many families, although you would be surprised how hard the private schools will work to help you find scholarships, grants and loans.

It's often very difficult to get the classes you need *when* you need them in order to graduate in four years from a public college or university. However, it's not uncommon for a student to earn a college degree at a private school in less than four years. Keep in mind that you can take summer school classes at your local public college, which can help you get some basic classes out of the way.

It may be important for you to attend a private school of considerable prestige. Maybe your parents graduated from an Ivy League school, and it's virtually expected that you will do the same. Family tradition often carries a lot of weight when it comes to choosing a college.

Big or Small

There are big differences between large and small colleges. You may think your high school was big with 3,000 students. Well, that's considered *small* when it comes to colleges. *Big* is a university the size of a medium-sized town. The pace is faster, the crowds bigger, and the options greater. That may get your blood pumping or it may scare you to death. You just have to investigate, which means talking to people who know the differences and personally visiting the campuses of your choice (see the section in this chapter called "Campus Visits").

Keep in mind that you will get more personal attention from your professors in a small school than a large one. A fact of higher education is that the larger the school, the more common it is for teaching assistants and graduate students to teach undergraduate courses. In smaller colleges the professors generally teach the classes.

Christian or Secular

The fastest growing category of higher education is the Christian college. More than a place to prepare for the ministry or to get training for missionary service, today's Christian colleges integrate the Christian worldview (see chapter 11) with a classic liberal arts education. There are even Christian universities that offer advanced degrees in business, nursing, computer science, psychology and art.

> According to recent statistics, undergraduate enrollment at colleges that are members of CCCU is increasing five times faster than other private colleges and all public institutions.

There are over 4,000 degree-granting institutions of higher education in the United States. Of those, approximately 1,600 are private, nonprofit campuses. About 900 of those private institutions claim to be "religiously affiliated" in some fashion. But only 105 institutions in the United States qualify for membership in the Council for Christian Colleges and

Seven Ways the Bible Would Have Been Different If It Had Been Written by College Students

1. The Last Supper would have been eaten the next morning—cold.

2. The Ten Commandments would actually only be five—double-spaced and written in a large font.

3. Forbidden fruit would have been eaten because it wasn't cafeteria food.

4. The reason Cain killed Abel would have been because they were roommates who disagreed over who would occupy the top bunk.

5. The end of the world would occur at finals, not Armageddon.

6. Moses and followers would have walked in the desert for 40 years because they didn't want to ask directions and look like freshmen.

7. Instead of creating the world in six days and resting on the seventh, God would have put it off until the night before it was due and then pulled an all-nighter.

Universities (www.cccu.org), because they are considered to be intentionally Christ-centered.

Should you consider a Christian college? We think you should (we admit to being biased, but in a good way). We're not saying that a Christian college is your only option, but it should definitely be an option if you already have a Christian worldview. Today's Christian college doesn't shelter you from competing philosophies, but rather it shows you how secular ideologies compare to God-centered truth.

Still, more Christian students attend secular colleges and universities than Christian colleges. And that's not a bad thing. Our secular institutions need the influence and witness of Christian kids, and you may need the specialized training that a secular institution can provide. You just need to be ready, willing and able to stand up to professors who will denounce your beliefs and students who will degrade your moral values (more about that later).

Campus Visits

Visiting the top schools on your list—especially if you've applied to them—is essential. The college you eventually choose—even if it's local—is going to be your home for at least the next year, and possibly the next four years. Contact the colleges on your list and arrange for a visit. Colleges can't wait to show off their campuses and have you meet their students and faculty. You and your parents should prepare ahead of time a list of what you want to see and questions you want to ask.

It's essential to tour the local community as well. If you're going to live off campus, check out the cost and quality of housing. Safety, both on and off campus, is always a big concern for parents, so ask about security issues.

Most colleges sponsor preview weekends for parents and students to go and look things over. These are great, but remember that if there's ever a time for a college to make everything look near perfect, this is it. Our suggestion is that you plan your own visit during the week (when classes are in session) and that you stay overnight, preferably in the dorm (this would be for you, not your parents). Talk to the students and ask direct questions. You'll get direct answers.

Making Your Final Choice

Ultimately you are the one who will have to decide where you're going to go to college. The best decision will come after you've done a lot of research, asked a lot of questions and done a lot of praying! Just in case you're still undecided, here are some wrong and some right reasons for choosing a college:

Bad Reasons to Choose a College

- The admissions counselor is a cool guy.
- The promotional literature and video are first rate.
- A bunch of your friends are going there.
- The beach (or mountains or lake or Krispy Kreme Doughnut shop) is less than 30 minutes away.
- This is the only school that accepted you (we're thinking of the famous line from Groucho Marx: "I'd never join a club that would have me as a member").

Good Reasons to Choose a College

- You discovered that the college has a strong program in your area of interest.
- You visited the campus, talked to some students and faculty, and even stayed in the dorm overnight.
- If you've chosen to attend a Christian college, you are confident that you will learn to inte-

grate your worldview into your area of study.

- If you've chosen to attend a secular college, you are aware of at least one strong Christian ministry on campus and you've already found a Bible-teaching church.

"Look, Toto, I Don't Think We're in High School Anymore"

The first couple of weeks of college are going to be a major learning experience for you in more ways than one. You think you're going to arrive and be cool from the very start. You've got these mental images of yourself cruising onto campus with a certain attitude that says, "Look out, world, here I am." Well, get that image out of your mind and picture yourself looking bewildered, befuddled and completely out of sync. This phenomenon befalls what used to be called a *freshman* but is now referred to as a *first-year student*.

A first-year student is one of the lowest forms of life, only slightly higher on the social scale than pond slime. You're like a green recruit going into the Marines for the first time. College administrators know this, of course, so they program your life for the first week or so.

You will stand in more lines and fill our more forms than you thought existed in the entire universe. You will go through registration, orientation, configuration and probably deterioration. You'll move into your room and meet your roommate (more about rooms and roommates in chapter 3), buy books, stock up on junk food, meet new people and check out the neighborhood (scoping out the local Denny's for those future midnight runs).

You're going to feel like a complete dweeb, but that's okay. The good news is that you won't stand out because all first-year students feel like dweebs.

It's Time for Class

Unlike when you were in high school, when your mommy woke you up and made sure you got to school on time, no one's going to wake you and dress you and send you out the door with a lunch pail and a kiss on the cheek, not even your roommate (if this happens, get a new roommate). The reason for this is simple: The college already has your money in its bank, so it has nothing to lose if you don't show up for class.

The size of your school will determine the size of your classes, but even small colleges sometimes throw undergraduate students together by the hundreds in those so-called survey classes, such as the History of the World 101, Old Testament Survey or the History of Pots and Pans. It's up to you not only to show up for class on time but also to develop good listening skills in these larger classes (staying awake is the first step to good listening).

Meet the Modern Professor

Unless you graduated from Sticks High School in rural Montana (sorry to be redundant), most of your nonsurvey classes will be smaller than your average high school classes. This is so you can have close interaction with the new authority in your life, the college professor.

Without college professors, college wouldn't exist. You go to college to learn, and professors are the ones who teach (it's amazing how many brilliant insights we come up with). College professors are supposed to be experts in their field of instruction, and for the most part that's true. In fact, you will find that most college professors are very dedicated to teaching you what they know so that you can graduate and be productive in your chosen field. There are some professors, however, who could care less about teaching and really don't care about you. Somewhere along the way, these people became cynical about life because they got mad at God—or perhaps because they were dropped on their heads as infants. Their only joy comes from contradicting the truth and making your life miserable.

The Difference Between "Eccentric" and "Arrogant"

When it comes to your professors, learn to distinguish between the eccentric and the arrogant. An *eccentric* professor wears Birkenstocks, appears absentminded and mumbles to himself. But he still loves to teach. An *arrogant* professor doesn't care about your questions and ultimately doesn't care about the truth. Enjoy eccentric professors, but avoid arrogant professors like the plague.

Keep in mind that your college professors are the new authorities in your life. They know it and you should, too.

Don't Believe Everything You're Taught

A college professor worth his or her salt doesn't expect you to believe everything you're taught. Some professors love to make shocking statements just to stimulate your thinking. Try not to act shocked or offended, even if you're going nuts inside. *Think it through*. What is your professor really saying and why? Do your homework and ask questions (hint: Be inquisitive but not annoying).

If a professor says something that offends your beliefs, don't react emotionally and don't take it personally. *Think it through*. Respond clearly and with respect, particularly if you are writing a paper.

Can You Learn from a Non-Christian Professor?

Absolutely! In fact, you may learn *more* about your faith than you ever thought possible. Just remember that when it comes to papers and tests, it's possible that some professors will mark any answer even remotely connected to God as wrong. On the other hand, don't leave your brains in your room just because your professor is a Christian. God may be simple to accept, but He's a complex Being with many mysteries. Avoid pat answers in any setting.

Moving On

In the next chapter we're going to tackle some of the issues involved in living on your own, whether you're in college or not. College can be a huge part of your life, but there's much more to these years than going to class and graduating. Remember that *real* success is more a matter of *who you are* than *what you do*.

Forwarding Address

Growing Up Usually Means Moving Out

I couldn't wait to leave home.
After I was gone for a while, I couldn't wait to go back.

ABBY T., AGE 21

If your home life is like most American households, there is a race going on in your family. The clock is ticking, and it is just a matter of time to see which happens first: Will you pack your bags and move out or will your parents pack your bags and throw you out?

Your parents are getting on your nerves. Go on, admit it. That doesn't mean you're a bad seed; it just means that you're going through the natural growth process of becoming an adult wanting more freedom. And since you're admitting things, why don't you admit that you are irritating your parents (as evidenced by those popped blood vessels in your father's eyeballs and the fact that your mother is losing clumps of hair from her scalp). It's reciprocal. You're driving them crazy and vice versa. That is one reason most people think about moving out after high school.

You'll quickly discover, however, that living away from your family's home isn't as glamorous as it seems. Sure, you won't have someone imposing a curfew or ordering lights out or demanding you to turn down the volume on your stereo. You won't even have anyone telling you that pizza is not a breakfast food. But living on your own may also mean you are literally on your own, buying food, paying rent, cooking, washing and doing a lot of other things that you never thought about before (because someone else was doing them for you).

Whether you are getting ready to move off to a dorm room at a university across the country or whether you just want to move down the block to that basement apartment with a hot plate for a kitchen and a bucket for a bathtub, this chapter is for you. We'll give you information that includes the good and the bad, the pros and the cons. When you read what we have to tell you, you'll still want to leave home, but you'll have a better idea of where you want to go (and a greater appreciation of what you're leaving behind).

Life on Your Own

From the time you were a little kid, you have been saying, "When I grow up . . ." Well, that time has arrived. You *have* grown up. During your four years of high school (more or less, depending on the level of your mental acuity), you gained a lot of experience in these areas:

- *Human Dynamics.* You developed friendships and interpersonal relationships (of the social, romantic and platonic types).
- *Finances.* You made small amounts of money and spent slightly more than that.
- *Communicative Skills.* You created intricate

excuses and presented persuasive rationalizations to your parents and teachers.

- *Cultural Sensitivity and Societal Awareness.* You watched a lot of television and movies.

With such worldly experience, it is no wonder that you are ready (even anxious) to leave the protective cover of your parents' roof and venture out on your own.

Your efforts to move out may be met with one horrendous roadblock: your parents. You see, they have a totally different view of you. It all stems from the fact that they used to powder your heinie. You were a baby back then, and they still consider you to be something less than a real adult. All of that experience that you gained during high school doesn't mean diddly-squat to them. If fact, what you think qualifies you to be an adult is what they consider to be proof that you are still a juvenile.

- *Human Dynamics.* They think that you are hanging out with a bunch of morons.
- *Finances.* They say that you have been living off the allowance they have been paying you. (You are tempted to remind them that $5 per week won't even buy a meal at Hot Dog on a Stick, but you actually need that financial subsidy,

so you can't afford to alienate yourself quite
yet.)

· *Communicative Skills.* They say that your conversation with them is always limited to
monosyllabic grunts (except when you fabri-
cate elaborate and outrageous excuses when
you are in trouble).

· *Cultural Sensitivity and Societal Awareness.* They
criticize you for watching a lot of television
and movies (as if that is a bad thing).

But you do have something working in your
favor. You are driving them crazy. They are tired of
the refrigerator door's being left open and the bathroom light's being left on. They are losing patience
with calls from your friends at 11:45 P.M. (That one is
their own fault; they should have gotten you the cell
phone you kept asking for.) They are totally frustrat-
ed with your habit of leaving clothes on your bedroom floor. (You think you're being efficient, because
you're not wasting time by opening and closing the
dresser drawers.) These parental irritations work in
your favor. Even though your parents don't consider
you to be an adult, by the time you're out of high
school they are somewhat anxious to get you out of
the house.

When to Go

The timing of when you make the break from your parents' home requires some strategy. Like a great actor in a theatrical play, take your bow and make your exit at a time when the audience wants you to return for an encore. In other words, when you leave, you want to make sure that your parents will let you come back.

There is a right time and a wrong time to leave home. It is the *wrong* time to leave when any of these are true:

- You've just had a huge fight with your parents, and Jerry Springer is calling to book you.
- You've just maxed out your parents' charge card, and you need to vanish before the invoice arrives.
- You don't have anyplace else to go to.

It is the *right* time to leave when these are true:

- You are in agreement with your parents that it is the right thing to do.
- There are no hard feelings between you and your parents.
- You are just beginning to consider their anti-quated opinions to be "quaint," and they are

just beginning to consider your irritating habits to be "endearing."

• You've got a great place to go to.

Your departure usually happens when you start college as a first-year student, but the specific timing will be determined by a lot of factors.

But I Don't Want to Go
What if you don't want to leave home? Well, you probably don't have to—at least not yet. But part of your growth process means stepping out into the world. That usually means living farther away from your parents than the bedroom across the hall.

What to Take with You
For the past 18 years, all of your worldly possessions have been stockpiled in your room. This arrangement was due to necessity (your parents didn't want your junk in the living room) and due to protection (you didn't want your younger siblings getting their grubby little hands on your stuff). When you leave home, you will be tempted to take all of your stuff with you. *Don't.* You won't need it all, and you won't have room for it anyway.

What to Leave Behind

We know that you are fond of that soccer trophy you won in the fifth grade, but that is a remembrance of the past that can stay behind. And if you are honest with yourself, you aren't all that sentimental about it (since for the last year you had a Jack in the Box antenna ball stuck on the soccer player's head). Your dorm room or apartment won't be much bigger than those photo booths at the mall where you can get four shots for a buck. With that in mind, plan to leave at home things such as these:

- Your high school yearbooks
- Your collections from childhood (such as comic books and troll dolls)
- Your favorite clothes from tenth grade, which you haven't worn since
- Your pets (goldfish might be the only exception, but not in that 30-gallon aquarium)

Remember that if you are just moving a short drive away to college, you can return home at another time to get what you need. (And if you are going so far away that you won't return home until summer break, then you really need to pack light.)

What to Take

If you are going away to college, then you will probably receive some information from the college about what you should bring. The obvious things will be on the list: a desk lamp for reading; a computer; a surge protector; towels and bed sheets (hey, you aren't staying at the Marriott Courtyard); and headphones for your stereo (so you won't disturb your roommate).

In addition, there are going to be a lot of things you haven't needed at home that you will need at college, such as a laundry basket, a small refrigerator and a few basic tools.

Coordinate the equipment list with your roommate. There is no sense in duplicating items.

Dorm Life

College is going to be filled with a lot of adjustments for you. You are going to be reading more and studying harder than you did in high school. But the academic transition is going to be easy compared with the tremendous adjustment to living in a dorm.

Think about it for a moment: Nothing in your lifetime of experience has equipped you for living in a dorm (unless you have 179 brothers and sisters). You'll have to make a number of adjustments—and quickly.

Instead of an older brother or sister, you'll have an RA (resident assistant). The RA will probably be a junior or senior. This person is paid to be your supervisor, mentor, counselor and warden. But don't think RAs are doing it only for the money. They usually get free room and board instead of cash. If you work that out on an hourly basis, their pay is about 27¢ per hour. So they're probably doing this job because they want to be helpful.

Instead of parents, you will have an RD (resident director). This could be a married couple or a graduate student. The RD is your best resource for heavier personal problems. (Your RA is okay, but not much older than you, so you might want to opt for a little more wisdom.)

Minimal privacy. Instead of sharing the bathroom with one or two siblings, you'll be looking at an average of about 16 people per toilet. You do the math.

Minimal quiet time. We're not talking about your morning devotions here. Instead of a "lights out" rule imposed by your parents, there will likely be activity throughout the night. At first you'll probably join in on the fun, but after four months of sleeping only three hours per night, your brain won't function and you will be constantly sick. (But don't worry about that runny nose—the bags under your eyes will be so droopy that you can wipe your nose with them.)

Survival Tips

A few weeks before the beginning of your first semester, you will be notified of the name, address and phone number of your roommate. Get acquainted by spending some time on the phone. Don't worry if you think you got stuck with a dud (your new roommate probably has a similar feeling). Don't even think about asking for a change in roommate assignments until you have both moved in and gotten to know each other.

You may be apprehensive about living with a complete stranger, but your roommate won't stay a stranger for long. Sure, you won't be totally compatible, but you lived at home and weren't totally compatible with your family members either.

Even if you shared a room with a sibling, the experience won't completely prepare you for living with a roommate. The rules for living with a roommate are slightly different. At home, your parents can arbitrate the disputes with your siblings; at college, you'll have to work things out on your own with your roommate (or with the help of your RA). The following perspectives may help:

• Don't think that your roommate has to be your best friend.

- Learn to appreciate your roommate's differences.
- Don't be too quick to borrow your roommate's stuff.
- When your roommate is starting to irritate you, remember that you may be doing things that irritate your roommate.
- Don't let the irritations build up to the point that you explode over something ridiculous (such as "I hate you, I hate you! You always hum when you comb your hair!").

Dining Commons

When you are at college, you'll probably eat most of your meals in a dining commons along with hundreds of people just like you. In chapter 8 we will discuss some guidelines for *what* to eat (so that you don't swell like an overinflated whoopee cushion after the first semester). For now we just want to remind you that table manners seem to be forgotten when people eat in scavenging hordes.

We aren't being critical, just observant. We know that you'll be foraging for food in a cafeteria line and eating off a tray. This is not a time to be lifting your pinkie as you sip your soup. But when you go home—or get invited to the university president's house for dinner—don't toss the peas into the air and catch them in your mouth.

A Little Privacy, Please

In order to maintain your sanity, you are going to have to find your own private "quiet place." This will be a place where you dodge all of the interruptions. It will be a place where you can talk with God and read your Bible; it will be a place where you can organize your thoughts; it will be a place where you can enjoy the quietness of silence. (And maybe you can do a little homework there, too.)

It may take you a while to find this special place. Look for an isolated, overstuffed chair in the library. Try to find a bench under a shade tree (preferably far away from the soccer practice field). If all else fails, try the backseat of your RA's car. Wherever it is, find this place and don't tell anyone about it until after you graduate.

Apartment Life

Life in an apartment has some similarities to living in a dorm, but there are some significant differences.

Furniture

Dorm rooms come furnished with beds, dressers and desks. But unless you rent an apartment that's furnished, the only features of your apartment will be wall-to-wall floors and see-through windows. You will be on your own for the furniture.

Your vivid imagination and your empty wallet will guide your decorating tastes. Who needs a bed frame when a mattress lies perfectly flat on the floor? The box that your 17-inch computer monitor came in will make an excellent dining table. You'll be amazed at what you can build out of "sticks and stones": A few pine boards stacked between concrete bricks make an excellent bookcase. Or if you want to go for the beach-comber motif, build two towers of bricks and lay a surfboard across the top. Presto! You've got an abstract breakfast counter.

Location, Location, Location

You might find a great apartment for a great price, but you'll have a problem if it is seven miles from campus and your only means of transportation is a pair of Nikes. Dorms are conveniently located, but this may not be the case with an apartment.

Remember that your college classes are not sched-uled in a row like in high school. You might have only two classes on Monday, Wednesday and Friday, but one is from 9:30 to 10:20, and the other from 1:15 to 2:05. Where are you going to go in the meantime? If your apartment is too far away, you might have a lot of wasted time between classes when you can't conveniently eat, sleep, shower or study. And if you have a car, then you have to think about parking (both at the apartment and on campus).

For your first year of college, living closer to campus is probably better than being farther away. Not only is it more convenient, but you'll also be able to participate in more of the social activities.

A Final Word of Caution for When You Leave Home

Before you make the official and final departure from your parents' house, take a good look around. For the first time you may notice the nice furniture, the clean surroundings and the well-stocked refrigerator. Don't make the mistake of asking your parents, "Why should I leave all of this?" One of them will quickly answer, "Because it is not yours!"

Moving On

When you are living in your parents' home, you play by their rules. Sometimes it is difficult to know "who you really are" when you're in that situation. What you think, do and say are strongly influenced by your parents' expectations.

All of that changes when you move away from home. Suddenly what you think, do and say are totally up to you. Your parents no longer dictate these things—your character determines them. That important subject, your character, is the focus of the next chapter.

Your Character

It's Who You Really Are

> *After high school, you'll find out what you really
> believe, because then it is all up to you.*
>
> CAROLYN C., AGE 20

After high school, it may feel as though you don't know who you are anymore.

Don't freak out. It isn't all bad—just part of the process. For 18 years you have been defined mostly by what your family does and says and believes. You have also been partly defined by the friends you hang around with. After high school—and particularly if you go away to college—you won't have your family and old friends around to define you. Your external environment may be different. But you are still the same person inside.

That can be hard to remember when everything starts changing so suddenly and drastically. The activities in your life will increase exponentially after high school. Unless you are careful, the "inner you" may get lost—or at least overlooked. If you're going to college, then the academic load will almost bury you; if you're working a job, you'll be physically and emotionally drained at the end of the day. If any time is left between your classes and your job, you'll be doing things and going places with your friends. In the midst of the flurry of activity, don't ignore the importance of developing your character.

The tough decisions in your life are not going to be decided by your looks or your personality or your intellect. The most difficult issues you'll face in life are going to be decided by your character.

What Is Character?

Character is the inward conviction of your beliefs that affects your outward behavior. Your character is the "real you." It is what you stand for—what you believe in. Your character is what may keep you from doing things you shouldn't and makes you do the right thing even when it is difficult.

What Does Character Look Like?

Unfortunately, you can't see character. You can't take a written test to quantify it. You will only know what your own character is like by examining your conduct in various circumstances. Your character is revealed by

- how you treat people who can do nothing for you;
- your ability to accept personal criticism without feeling malice toward the person who gives it;
- your response when you suddenly lose a lot of money—and when you suddenly acquire a lot of money;
- the kinds of things that make you angry;

- the kinds of things that make you laugh;
- how you respond to temptation;
- what you stand for and what you won't stand for;
- what you fall for and what you lie for;
- what you do with what you have;
- what you do when you have nothing to do;
- what you do when you know nobody will ever find out.

> *Reputation* is what you need to get a job.
> *Character* is what you need to keep it.

Essential Ingredients

During high school, there were probably times when your character was tested. As difficult as those circumstances might have been, the temptations and pressure to compromise your character will increase dramatically after high school. You need to be serious about developing and strengthening your character so that you will be able to stand firm in the confidence of what you believe.

Some men and women (Billy Graham and Mother

Teresa, for example) are universally recognized for their character. These people are known for consistently exemplifying sound moral character. If you find it hard to imagine living up to such lofty standards, take heart. Character is not something acquired genetically; nor is there a "one size fits all" formula for character development. It takes time—and a fair amount of effort.

Where do you begin? Well, this list of desirable character traits is not intended to be exhaustive, but if you are working on your own character, these are good traits to start with:

- *Integrity*—doing what is right
- *Honesty*—being truthful
- *Responsibility*—being trustworthy
- *Morality*—being pure in thought and deed

There Is More to the Definition

Look at the brief definitions that we have given to the character traits of integrity, honesty, responsibility and morality. Now for each one of them, add the following phrase: "all of the time, in every situation, regardless of the consequences." That is what *character* is all about.

Character is always lost when a high ideal is sacrificed on the altar of conformity and self-interest.

Sometimes it is easier to exhibit character when faced with big temptations than it is when faced with seemingly insignificant ones. If a bank teller left a stack of $20 bills on the counter, we could resist the momentary temptation to take it (and feel pleased with ourselves for the display of honesty). But what about when the McDonald's "customer service associate" hands us 25¢ too much in change? All of a sudden our honesty evaporates because we think it is too small or that it doesn't matter. But the essence of character is that it operates all of the time and in every situation.

True character operates regardless of the consequences. It is easy to deal honestly with the faults of others. But what about when you are on the hot seat? This is the real test of character. Do you have the integrity to own up to your own mistakes, even when it might mean that you suffer some penalty or disadvantage? Don't let your pride squelch your character.

Is It Okay to Laugh?

Does this all-character, all-of-the-time approach mean that life will be boring? Absolutely not! We think that people with strong character can have the best sense of humor. Because they have decided what must be taken absolutely seriously, they are free to take everything else lightly.

A strong faith in God gives you assurance to stand firm in your convictions regardless of the consequences. When you are trusting God with the circumstances of your life, you don't need to worry about compromising your character in order to maneuver the situation.

Most people take "ethical detours" when they think that they have to strategize or control the outcome of events. But when you realize that God is in control, you are relieved of the temptation to violate your principles in order to manipulate the results.

What you believe affects the way you think.
The way you think affects the way you live.

Live in the Truth

The Bible is filled with verses that extol the importance of having strong character. Because we are dads, we can really relate to the following verse in the New Testament:

> I could have no greater joy than to hear that my children live in truth (3 John 4).

We *suspect* that your parents feel the same way. We *know* that your heavenly Father feels that way.

Living in truth is living your life with Christlike character. That's what the Christian life is all about. God wants us to become like His Son (see Romans 8:29). If you think that such a goal is impossible, you're right: It is (in this lifetime at least). Even the apostle Paul struggled with character issues:

> I know I am rotten through and through so far as my old sinful nature is concerned. No matter which way I turn, I can't make myself do right. I want to, but I can't. When I want to do good, I don't. And when I try not to do wrong, I do it anyway (Romans 7:18-19).

We will never achieve perfect Christlike character on this earth. That will only happen when we are united with Christ when He returns (see 1 John 3:2). In the meantime, we can follow biblical principles for living in truth.

Living in truth begins with transformed thinking. Our society doesn't place much value on virtue. It teaches that ethics is a private matter and that morality is relative. You could never develop strong character while having the philosophy that there is nothing worth believing in. The apostle Paul said that living for God requires a complete change in your mind-set:

> Don't copy the behavior and customs of this world, but let God transform you into a new person by changing the way you think. Then you will know what God wants you to do, and you will know how good and pleasing and perfect his will really is (Romans 12:2).

Living in truth is sustained by consistent conduct. Your character isn't going to be developed if you only exercise it on Sundays and religious holidays. Character is strengthened over the course of many acts, and it can be severely weakened by repeated compromise. Living in truth requires consistent and persistent focus on those things that are good, right and true. Here are the apostle Paul's instructions to stay focused and consistent in life:

> And now, dear friends, let me say one more thing as I close this letter. Fix your thoughts on what is true and honorable and right. Think about things that are pure and lovely and admirable. Think about things that are excellent and worthy of praise (Philippians 4:8).

Living in truth realizes God's present *purpose.* You may find it easier to live in truth when you realize that God wants to be active and alive in you right now. He has a present plan and purpose for your life. He doesn't intend to put your life on hold for a few years until you finish college or get settled in a career. He wants to use you now. This reason alone should give you great motivation to live in truth.

> **Your *reputation* can be damaged
> by the opinion of others.
> Only you can damage your *character*.**

Learn from Those Around You

One of the best ways to learn about character and to develop your own is to examine the lives of others. Of course, you will find many examples in the pages of the Bible, not the least of which is Christ Himself. But you have lots of living examples around you. Sometimes the character of these people inspires us; other times, their lapses in character serve as a warning to us.

Heroes

Okay, we want to be very clear about this. We aren't talking about superheroes (the kind in comic books, TV shows or movies). And we certainly aren't talking about celebrities (of either the sports or entertainment variety). We're talking about real-life heroes—people who exemplify our ideals and whose lives exhibit our highest values.

There is nothing wrong with having a hero. Heroes embody the character that we want to have. The best candidates for "hero" status are people who are dead (because a little history has to pass before the person's character is recognized and remembered). Even though these people were far from perfect, they refused to let their frailties prevent them from using their strengths. When we think of them, we should not focus on their imperfections or their accomplishments, but we should admire the traits of their character.

Your heroes might be famous (Abraham Lincoln, Eleanor Roosevelt, George Washington Carver, Amelia Earhart), or they could be obscure (if we could give you an example, then they wouldn't be obscure). Fame is not the important quality of heroes; instead, the diligence of their pursuit of what's right in the face of adversity is what matters.

Role Models

There is a big difference between heroes and role models.

- *Role models are people you see on a regular basis.* Heroes are admired from a distance (usually because they have been dead for generations).
- *Role models show you how things actually get done.* Heroes inspire you with ideals and concepts.
- *Role models show the techniques.* Heroes are the philosophy.

Both heroes and role models will be helpful in character formation, but you will get the most practical assistance from the role model.

Don't expect to find a role model who is famous. (Famous people probably won't be hanging around where you can see them.) Besides, fame isn't a necessary criteria for a good role model. You are only interested in finding someone who is a few stages ahead of you and who is managing life in a way that you admire.

You want a role model who is successful (in terms of quality of his or her character and life). Maybe this will be a person at your church or a supervisor where you work. Watch what they do, and see how they respond to circumstances. If you are going to college, your role model might be a senior who is doing well academically and is heavily involved in social issues. Perhaps you admire the way this senior is able to keep everything in balance. Don't be afraid to ask a few questions and receive a few practical pointers.

Speaking of practical pointers, when you are looking for a role model, find someone who has a personality and talents that are similar to your own. It won't work if you try to emulate the work habits of a person who is totally different from yourself.

Mentors

A mentor is different from both a hero and a role model. Mentoring involves an advising and counseling relationship that includes some accountability. A mentor is someone who will commit to be a personal "coach" to you.

Mentors won't seek you out; you must approach them. In fact, beware of the person who is too anxious to be your mentor (a kook in search of a groupie). A serious mentoring relationship takes a lot of time, but your mentor will be willing to make such a commitment to you if you show a sincere interest in learning and growing. Maybe one of your church leaders or a professor at college would be a good mentor for you.

You Gotta Be You

The bottom line: Your character is between you and God. It cannot be purchased, inherited or borrowed from someone else. You can get help, advice, instruction and inspiration from the Bible, your heroes, role models and mentors, but the responsibility of developing your character belongs entirely to you. Take this job seriously.

Handling Your Free Time

One of the first tests of your character after high school will be how you handle the seemingly unlimited freedom that is available to you. If your character is strong, you can avoid wasting and abusing your free time. If your character is weak, you'll have lots of wasted time and nothing to show for it.

For your entire life through high school, the time frame of your life was fairly rigid. Your daily routine probably went something like this:

- You begin the day by turning off the alarm clock and going back to sleep.
- Next, you hear a parent yelling, "You've overslept! Get out of bed!" You go back to sleep.
- You finally get out of bed, skipping shower and breakfast, and sneak into the first-period class as the sound waves of the tardy bell are dissipating.
- For the next seven hours, you respond to class bells, moving in zombielike fashion between classes.
- After the school dismissal bell, it's a few hours of some job, sport or activity, according to the schedule imposed by your employer, coach, advisor or parent.
- You eat a generic dinner before driving to some activity with the church youth group or with friends. You arrive home after curfew (but not so late as to get into *real* trouble with your parents), and you fall asleep after setting

the alarm clock for a time earlier than you know you will really get up.

When you think of it this way, your entire life seems controlled by adults and bells.

After high school, all of that changes. Oh, there are still adults and bells around, but they don't control your life unless you allow them to. Your daily routine could go something like this:

- You begin the day by awakening peacefully. No alarm sounded because you didn't set the clock. It is noon. You go back to sleep.
- Next, you awake in time for an afternoon snack while watching a few *Saved by the Bell* reruns.
- A leisurely dinner with friends at Taco Bell is followed by a movie and then a fruit smoothie at the Jamba Juice joint. You catch Leno and Letterman and fall asleep during Conan.

Now, doesn't this sound much more serene? No stress with this lifestyle—not until you flunk out of school, lose your job and are evicted from your apartment.

You can know all of the best time management

principles (see chapter 1), but your character must be strong enough to motivate you to use them.

Moving On

Now that we have talked about character, let's move to the subject that will likely be the greatest challenge to your character or the greatest help to it—your friends.

As you already know from personal experience, some of your friends encourage you to live a life that is consistent with your character; other friends may pressure you to compromise your character. As we'll discuss in the next chapter, the choice is up to you. Choose wisely.

Friends

Choose or Lose

You think you will always stay close with your best friends from high school. That probably won't happen. After high school, you'll meet lots of new people and will probably develop more meaningful, deeper friendships with some of them. Don't think that you are a bad person when this happens. It is natural.

PETER N., AGE 22

Your personal character and integrity aren't the only factors that determine the kind of person you'll become. There's an outside influence you've got to consider: *people.*

We don't mean just *any* people—like your roommate or the people down the hall or your parents or your professors or your employers. These are the people you're stuck with, for better or for worse. (C'mon, it's not that bad.) We're talking about people who are much more fun, much more special and much more influential. We're talking about your *friends.*

Ah, friends. They're probably a very important part of your life right now. Your friends have always been there for you. They basically got you through high school. Unlike your family, who want to change you, your friends accept you for who you are, just the way you are. They don't judge you. No wonder the wisest man who ever lived said, "A real friend sticks closer than a brother" (Proverbs 18:24).

To get you started, we want to give you a few tips on how to form friendships. We're going to start with the most important friend you'll ever have, and work our way down from there.

The Greatest Friend in the World

There are several criteria you could use to choose friends. In fact, we're going to ask you to place the following qualities of friendship in order of importance:

__ Has a cool car
__ Gives you lecture notes when you don't go to class
__ Has your best interest in mind all the time
__ Buys beer for you
__ Forgives you no matter what you have done
__ Loans you that cool car
__ Loans you money
__ Knows you better than anyone else

How does your list look? What's the number one quality you look for in a friend? Wouldn't it be great to have a friend who knows you better than anyone else? Well, guess what? You already do. His name is God.

Now, you may not believe us, because you probably think God has a lot more important things to do than be your friend (like run the universe). Yes, God is very involved in our world, but His first priority is you. You don't have to just take our word for it. Here's what the Bible says about God's knowing you:

Not even a sparrow, worth only half a penny, can fall to the ground without your Father knowing it. And the very hairs on your head are all numbered. So don't be afraid; you are more valuable to him than a whole flock of sparrows (Matthew 10:29-31).

This isn't fairy tale stuff. The God who knows everything (it's called *omniscience*) and can do anything (that's called *omnipotence*) knows *you* completely. And here's the kicker: Even though He knows everything about you, He still loves you unconditionally. "This is real love. It is not that we loved God, but that he loved us" (1 John 4:10).

Make Friends with Your Family

So far in this book we've talked a lot about leaving home. Even if you aren't leaving home in a physical sense, you are in the process of leaving as you take on more responsibility for yourself. You will always be a part of your family and your heritage. You can never truly leave your family, no matter how much you'd like to at times.

Even though it might seem as though your family wants to run your life, you need to embrace your family as your friends. We've put this category of friend-ship right below God in importance, because no other earthly friendships will be more important to you.

This includes your parents and grandparents, your siblings, your uncles and aunts, and your cousins. If and when you get married, your spouse and your chil-dren and eventually your grandchildren will become your best friends.

Perhaps you don't feel this way about your family. At this stage in your life, your friends may mean more to you than your family. Believe us when we say that your friends will come and go, but your family will always be there. Blood really is thicker than water.

What If Your Family Is Dysfunctional, Abusive or Irresponsible?

You may come from a family with real problems. We aren't experts in the field of dysfunctional families; if you need help to figure out how to handle your par-ticular family situation, your pastor or priest may be able to direct you to someone who can help.

There is one thing we can tell you for sure, howev-er. There is a way to overcome your family challenges, and it's not going to come from trying to change them. The greatest thing you can do is to love your family members where they are and pray for them every day.

Our good friend and mentor John Trent has written about his relationship with his father, which was difficult for as long as he knew his father. John never stopped loving his dad, even on his father's deathbed, when he still refused to give John his approval. John never let his father's dysfunction stand in the way of his own success and his responsibility before God, but he also never stopped loving and respecting his father.

Your Pastor Is A Friend Who Guides You

We all need spiritual leaders in our lives, people ordained by God to watch over us and to pray for us. If you have never made friends with your pastor or priest, you are missing out on an incredibly rich friendship. If you've never been in the habit of going to church, now would be a great time to start (more about church in chapter 11).

Especially if you are away from home, you need the stability and accountability of a church. You need to be around people who care about your spiritual needs. When you find a church, introduce yourself to the pastor. If the church is very large, you should get to know the associate pastor or the college pastor. Tell your pastor or priest that you want to form a friendship. "Remember your leaders who first taught you the word of God. Think of all the good that has come from their lives, and trust the Lord as they do" (Hebrews 13:7).

Look for Friends Who Are Friends with God

After God, your family and your pastor, the most important friends you can have are friends who are friends with God.

We're not saying you should never make friends with people who aren't Christians. To the contrary, as a Christian, part of your mission in the world is to make friends with people who don't know God personally. We're just saying that you should make it a priority to seek out Christian friends first. Before you can hope to be a positive influence on others, you need people around you who will be a positive influence on you.

We admit that finding these kinds of friends may not be as easy as it sounds. How do you find quality friends? Where do you look? What do you look for?

How to Find Forever Friends

Here's the best formula we know for developing long-lasting friendships:

To *find* good friends, you need to *be* a good friend.

You can't necessarily pick your friends and then expect them to fall in line, willing to be your friend. It's a lot more effective to *be* the kind of friend you are looking for in others.

In the classic book *The Friendship Factor*, Dr. Alan Loy McGinnis lists these five ways to deepen your relationships:

1. *Assign top priority to your relationships.* Don't be a fair-weather friend, or a part-time friend. It's better to be a good friend to a few people than a lousy friend to many.
2. *Cultivate transparency.* There isn't one personality trait that defines a good friend, but there is one quality that does: openness. If you aren't willing to be open and honest with your friends, then you aren't really a friend.

3. *Dare to talk about your affection.* By "affection," Dr. McGinnis means warmth more than he means physical attraction. A true friend is a caring friend.

4. *Learn the gestures of love.* Demonstrate consideration, kindness and giving, which should take place in a true friendship as well as in a marriage relationship.

5. *Create space in your relationship.* Dr. McGinnis writes that the tendency to control others "gets the prize for ruining more relationships than any other." If you want to be a good friend, give your friends room. Jealousy is a nasty trait in any relationship.[1]

What to Do About Negative Influences

There's a chance that as you've been reading this book, you realized that you've already made some poor choices in friends. You may have even broken off some lousy friendships from high school, but you're already back under the negative influence of some new friends.

First of all, the fact that you're thinking about

your poor choices is a good thing. Maybe you will be less likely to repeat your mistakes in the future. For now—and the sooner you do this the better—here's what to do:

- Avoid the friends that have a negative influence on you (they won't miss you).
- Don't abandon a good friend going bad. Confront him or her in a loving way.
- If your words have no affect, be willing to cut the ties, but continue to pray for your friend.

What About Fraternities and Sororities?

We've got to admit that neither of us has any experience with the Greeks on campus (geeks, yes; Greeks, no). So we can only tell you what we've heard and read.

Fraternities and sororities are a time-honored tradition in North American colleges and universities. Many a successful person can trace his or her strength as a student, and later as a graduate, to a fraternity or sorority. We're told that fraternity brothers and sorority sisters make friends for life.

That doesn't mean that you have to join a Greek

club if you want lifelong friends and valuable business contacts. We're just pointing out one of the benefits often cited by Greek advocates.

On the negative side, fraternities and sororities seem to receive more than their share of publicity over the problem of drinking. Truthfully, the connection between college students and alcohol goes way beyond fraternities and sororities. The problem on campuses is so acute that many colleges and universities are finally waking up and doing something to curb drinking, especially the deadly practice of binge drinking.

The question you have to ask yourself is this: Is it wise to put yourself in a position where you will be continuously exposed to alcohol (or drugs or tobacco), which not only will damage your body but could also impair your relationships with others, including God? Or would it be better to live in an environment that encourages you to do the right thing, whether it's in the spiritual, moral or intellectual part of your life?

Yes, There Are Christian Fraternities and Sororities

If you just have to be a Greek, why not check out one of the many Christian Greek houses located around the country. One of the oldest and best-known fraternities is Alpha Gamma Omega, a national Christ-centered organization. Founded on the campus of UCLA in 1927, AGO has chapters on several college campuses (AGO's website is www.ago.org). AGO's motto is Fraternity for Eternity.

You Can Influence Others

Here's an exciting thought for you as you enter your career as a college student:

> Wherever you are, God wants to use you to influence others.

The last message Jesus gave to His followers was to "go into all the world and preach the Good News to everyone, everywhere" (Mark 16:15). You see, as a Christ-follower, your job is to be a *witness* for Christ wherever you are in the world. Right now, whether you're in college or working in a job or both, Christ is asking you to tell others about Him.

Yes, you need to build your friendship network by first finding friends who share your values. But don't isolate yourself in a Christian comfort zone (this is especially true if you are at a Christian college). Follow the example of Christ, who did not shy away from people who were considered undesirable by the religious elite.

Don't make friends with people in order to share or endorse their lifestyle. Rather, make friends in order to influence them for Christ. Like the apostle Paul, you and your Christian friends should see yourselves as "Christ's ambassadors" (2 Corinthians 5:20), believing that God is using you to speak to your non-Christian friends. Remember that if you identify yourself with Christ, then you represent Him with your words, your actions and your attitudes.

Whether you are dealing with your roommate, a professor, a fraternity brother or sorority sister, a coworker or a new friend in class, you need to know that you may be the best ambassador for Christ that this person has ever encountered. And just so you won't feel any unnecessary pressure, you need to also know that it is Christ in you—not you—who will draw others to Christ. Because you are willing to be used by God, your life will be like "a fragrance presented by Christ to God" (2 Corinthians 2:15).

Because you are Christ's ambassador, you will inevitably get questions from your non-Christian friends—questions related to God and the peace of heart and mind that you radiate. Don't be *afraid* of these questions. Be *ready* to answer them.

If you are asked about your Christian hope, always be ready to explain it. But you must do this in a gentle and respectful way (1 Peter 3:15-16).

Radical Lifestyles

During your college years it is a virtual certainty that you will encounter an array of lifestyles unlike anything you have ever seen (notice we said "encounter" rather than "experience"). But here's the amazing part. If you are a Christian in a secular college, intent on living out your faith, *you* are going to be the one pegged as *radical*. Your lifestyle of living for Christ is going to be an affront and will appear "foolish" to those living in darkness. But don't despair and don't condemn. Instead, draw strength from the wisdom of Paul in the Bible:

I know very well how foolish the message of the cross sounds to those who are on the road to destruction. But we who are being saved recognize this message as the very power of God (1 Corinthians 1:18).

A Friend to the Friendless

Wherever you go throughout your life, you're going to

meet the friendless. These are the outcasts, the odd-balls, the strange. When high school students cruelly exclude and ridicule these outcasts, their behavior can be partially explained as ignorant or misguided. But full-fledged adults have no such excuse. If you deliberately contribute to the exclusion of another human being from your little group of friends for no other reason than that they're "different," shame on you.

Instead of excluding, try including the loner, the unlovely and the unusual person. Don't force it, but do your best to uncover the inner beauty and intrinsic value of that person. Become a friend to the friendless.

Home for the Holidays

There will come a time during your first few months away from home that you will return home—probably for Thanksgiving or Christmas. This is a grand occasion for three reasons:

1. You will get some home cooking for a change.
2. Everybody will be glad to see you.
3. You'll have an opportunity to show your family and old friends how much you have changed—for the better.

The easiest thing in the world would be to pick up where you left off by running with the same old friends and slipping back into your old habits. But that would also be a big mistake. It's not that you're suddenly better than everyone back home. You don't want to give the people you know the impression that "the fancy college boy is too good for us now."

Pray and ask God to give you a humble and grateful spirit as you go home. Stand firm in your convictions and your new pattern of associating with quality friends, but still show consideration and love to your old friends who seek you out. And if by chance someone asks you, "What happened? You seem different," be ready to give an answer that just might change their life.

Moving On

We could go on and on about friends and friendships—as a matter of fact, we will! In the next chapter we're going to talk about friendships that go beyond the casual to something more meaningful and challenging.

More Than Friends

Dating and Beyond

Guys shouldn't think that a girl will expect him to marry her if he takes her on one date.

JENNIFER B., AGE 21

It's almost a sure thing that sometime in your post-high-school career, you and a member of the opposite sex will find each other attractive. It will be hard to explain, because it will involve a combination of your physical, mental, emotional and spiritual dimensions. This won't be new for you, since you probably experienced this attraction in high school.

But now that you're on your own, on the verge of becoming a full-fledged adult, with all the privileges and rights therein, you'll want to treat this guy-girl thing with more respect and responsibility. In fact, we have a little theory about this guy-girl thing. Try this on for size (by the way, feel free to apply our theory to situations other than relationships, such as scuba diving and surgery):

The deeper you go, the more responsible you must become.

You're probably going to have more than one serious relationship over the next few years, and you may end up in a relationship with someone you are convinced is "the one." The key is that in each relationship, you need to show respect and practice responsibility. And the more serious you get in each relationship, the more responsible you must become.

Are You Leaving Someone Behind?

If you're leaving home, you could be leaving someone special behind. Or the two of you may be taking different paths as you enter your college years. Either way, how do you break things up gracefully—or should you break up at all?

We know a young man who had just graduated from high school and was leaving home for college. He had a sweet girlfriend in his hometown, who was still in high school. We were very impressed with how this guy handled this difficult situation. Because God was at the center of their relationship while they were dating, this young man kept God at the center when they broke up. Why did they break up at all? He felt it was important for each of them to meet new people and experience new things. Taking the lead, he prayed with his girlfriend, committing their futures to God. Though parting was difficult, they both knew they were doing the right thing.

At last report, the young man is enjoying his college experience very much, and his former girlfriend is successfully finishing high school.

On the other hand, we have known Christian couples who went off to different schools (in some cases they agreed to see other people; in other cases not) only to wind up together. Pray about what God has in store for you, both individually and as a couple, and be open to the direction in which God is leading you both.

If you're not willing to be responsible, then you shouldn't get serious. Going deeper in any relationship without practicing responsibility shows no respect for the other person or for yourself. And ultimately you show no respect for God.

> Love is patient and kind. Love is not jealous or boastful or proud or rude. Love does not demand its own way. Love is not irritable, and it keeps no record of when it has been wronged. It is never glad about injustice but rejoices whenever the truth wins out. Love never gives up, never loses faith, is always hopeful, and endures through every circumstance (1 Corinthians 13:4-7).

Dating 201

You were probably wondering when we were going to mention the magic word: *dating*. Now that we have, let's talk about what we mean. In case you hadn't noticed, the concept of dating has gone through a revolution of sorts. A lot of people have tried to redefine dating, while others have avoided the subject altogether. We're not going to take that position. We're going to deal with dating head-on, because we happen to think it's a very good idea.

Now that you're at the college level, you're ready to move up in your dating courses. In high school you took Dating 101, an introductory class. Here you learned—through trial and error—the rudiments of being with a guy or girl on a date. What kind of grade did you get in Dating 101? If you got a C or better, you're ready to move on. If you failed, or if you never took the class at all, we're going to promote you anyway. We don't want you to get any further behind.

Kiss Dating Hello?

A few years ago a best-selling book encouraged singles to "kiss dating goodbye." The author contended that, since it's very difficult to practice dating while remaining physically, emotionally and spiritually pure, it's best to avoid dating altogether until you're ready to make a commitment to one person for life in a marriage relationship.

We agree that it's important to put God first in every aspect of life, including every relationship we cultivate.

However, we also think that to avoid dating altogether is a bit extreme. It puts undue pressure on those who are in dating relationships to make a marriage commitment before they are ready—emotionally, financially or experientially.

When done responsibly, dating can make you a better person. Dating helps you relate to the opposite sex (which you'll have to do all your life, even if you never get married). And there are more benefits of dating.

Why Date?

Our being old enough to be your parents has its advantages when we discuss this topic of dating. For one thing, we've done a lot of dating (we got to know our wives on dates before we married them, and we continue to date because they continue to enjoy our "social engagements"). In addition, we have been able to observe our own kids through the high school and college years as they have dated. As a result of this dating experience, both as participants and observers, we have seen several benefits to dating:

- Dating civilizes you.
- Dating develops your social skills.
- Dating teaches you how to live on a budget.

- Dating shows you how the opposite sex thinks and feels.
- Dating helps you determine the kinds of qualities you enjoy in another person.

Dating doesn't have to be the prelude to anything more, but we think dating is a necessary prerequisite to growing deeper in an honest and honorable relationship with someone of the opposite sex. Dating helps you cultivate valuable and special friendships without worrying about the pressure of permanent commitment. If and when you are ready to commit yourself in marriage, you will have already learned a lot about understanding and caring for your future husband or wife.

A Balanced Approach to Dating

By now we hope you've noticed a definite theme running through this book (and frankly, we hope it's a theme that runs through your life). The theme is *balance*. Whether we're talking about your

- becoming the person God wants you to be,
- choosing the best friends possible,
- maintaining a healthy lifestyle,
- keeping your finances in order,

• selecting the career that's best for you, or
• entering the world of dating,

one of the keys to your success is *balance*.

We're not talking *boring mediocrity* here. Ask professional people—athletes, musicians, entertainers, scientists, business people—and they'll give you the same advice. If you keep a balanced perspective, seeking the best in all areas, maintaining a solid position and learning from the successes (and mistakes) of others, you will succeed yourself—and have fun doing it.

When it comes to dating, balance means you don't get caught up in a dating frenzy, where you're running ragged or where you're putting yourself in potentially compromising positions (and we think you know what we mean). But neither are you isolating yourself in your room or hiding behind the dynamics of a group, afraid to get close to anyone. Yes, you may have been hurt in the past, and the last thing you want is another relationship. Maybe you're so busy that the last thing you have time for is dating. Maybe you want to date, but nobody's asking, or everyone you ask turns you down.

Be patient. The right person will come along—if not for life, then for your next date! In the meantime, take the pressure off yourself. Enjoy your friends and relax. But don't stop reading here. The dating tips ahead will come in handy someday (and maybe sooner than you think). And if you're ready today—heck, you may be heading out the door for a date in the next 30 minutes—read fast. The next few paragraphs will help keep you balanced.

Treat Every Date with Respect

You never know. The next person you date may turn out to be your spouse (we don't mean to scare you). It's true! At some point you're going to meet for the first time the person you're going to marry someday. Or if that isn't the case, then you're likely to meet the person who will marry someone else someday. So treat every date with respect. See him or her as God's choice for someone (that someone could be you) or as someone who will eventually choose to remain purely single.

Something to Think About

You're at the age when many people meet their lifetime marriage partner. So it's a good idea to avoid getting into a long-term relationship with anyone who

- isn't your type,
- isn't good for you,
- doesn't share your values, or
- doesn't want to get married.

Discover Whether You're Compatible

Discovering whether you're compatible with someone seems like a catch-22. You don't want to seriously date someone with whom you're not compatible. But how can you tell whether you're compatible without dating that person?

Well, we can't help you identify specific personality characteristics ahead of time (that's one of the benefits of dating—to bring out the annoying or endearing habits in the other person). But before you can tell whether you are compatible with someone else, you need to know a few things about *yourself.* You should be able to answer yes to these three questions before you even begin to date someone:

- Do you know yourself? (See chapter 1.)
- Do you know God? (See chapter 5.)
- Does the person you want to date know God? (See 2 Corinthians 6:14.)

Take It Slowly

When it comes to developing deeper relationships, you will never regret taking your time. What you *will* regret is rushing into something that quickly turns out to be a mismatch. What you may find is that you relate to someone on a superficial level (read, physical), but then you discover over time that in the areas that really matter—spiritual depth, emotional stability, basic personality—you really aren't compatible at all.

Taking it slowly means that you meet somewhere for coffee or a coke and get to know each other before going out on an official date. It means going out in a group before going out alone. It means that after you get to know your new special someone a little, you evaluate whether or not you are truly compatible in the areas that matter. If you find at any point that either you or your special friend possesses qualities that the other would find intolerable, you need to have the courage and the character to prevent your relationship from moving beyond friendship.

But Don't Take Too Long

Now we get to the flip side of this whole relationship process, and that's *commitment* (at this point, all the guys reading this book are cringing, while the girls are saying, "Yesss!").

The opposite of rushing into a relationship—especially a marriage relationship—is never wanting to commit. This seems to be a pretty big problem right now, especially among men. There are a variety of reasons for this growing reluctance to commit to one person, especially when that commitment inevitably leads to marriage.

- *You may be from a broken home.* Rather than seeing marriage as a blessed union of souls, you see it as a battleground to be avoided at all costs.
- *You may be fearful of the financial uncertainty* that lies ahead in the world, not to mention your own bank account. You're still paying off student loans—from junior high school.
- *You're concentrating on your career.* You are on a course of study that's going to take a while, and after that it's going to take some time to establish your career.
- *You love playing the field.* Why settle down with one person, when that one person will only tie you down?
- *You're afraid of intimacy.* You just can't see yourself totally open and honest with another person.

We're not saying these are bad reasons for avoiding commitment. You just need to be aware of them and face up to the fact that any one of these reasons may be preventing you from entering into one of the most satisfying and enriching experiences available to us mere mortals (you can tell we're biased).

Dating can and should be fun, especially right now. Don't put any unnecessary pressure on yourself, and don't put any pressure on the person you're dating. Nothing kills a relationship quicker than when one of you seems too eager to get married. Be thoughtful and deliberate about dating, but enjoy the experience as you let it take its natural course. If God has placed in your heart a desire to get married, then rest in the confidence that dating is the best way to discover the person you will eventually fall in love with and marry.

Sexual Purity— It's Your Choice

We get a lot of e-mails from our readers (and we'd love to get one from you—see the introduction of the book for our address). One e-mail we received was from a young lady who was a new Christian. She told us that her boyfriend, who encouraged her to become a Christian, was upset when she told him, "No more sex!" He reasoned that they could be Christians and love each other and have sex. She was torn and confused. Here's what we advised.

Dear Torn and Confused—
 The Bible is very clear that sex outside of marriage is wrong. No way around that one. Check out

Proverbs 6:32 and 1 Corinthians 6:18. It's not that God doesn't want us to enjoy sex. But He created sex to be a sacred and very personal expression of love between a husband and wife. Anything outside of that is not only wrong but also destructive. This may sound old-fashioned, but you don't have to think very much to realize that nothing good—aside from temporary physical pleasure—comes from sex outside of marriage.

It's interesting that your boyfriend is the one who encouraged you to become a Christian, and yet he is upset that you won't have sex with him anymore. Doesn't it make you wonder about his love and respect for you? Take God out of the picture for a minute (your boyfriend has). If your boyfriend's main objective in having a relationship with you is sex, then you don't have much of a relationship. And please don't fall for the old line, "If you really love me, you'll have sex with me." If he really loves you, he'll respect you and honor you rather than seeing you as a physical object to meet his own selfish and misdirected desires.

Your salvation isn't based on what you have done or on what you will do. It's based on the love and work of Jesus Christ on your behalf (see Ephesians 2:8-10). But as you grow in Christ, you are going to find that you will want to please Him in all you do. That doesn't mean you won't fail. We all do. But there is a way out. It's not in our own abilities, but in Christ's. Only Jesus Christ can get you through this. Pray that He will give you strength and wisdom and courage.

Moving On

We've taken you farther down your life path than you probably need to go right now, but that's okay. It doesn't hurt to think ahead. When it comes to your future, plan as if it depends on you, but pray and trust God as if it depends on Him.

Now we're going to backtrack a bit to a more practical matter: *money*.

Money Matters

Your Fiscal Fitness Program

It will seem like you are spending more and more on less and less, until you are broke because you spent everything on nothing.

TIM P., AGE 22

Admit it. Until now, money hasn't been that much of a problem for you. Sure, there were times when you were running short. Maybe you couldn't go to the movie with your friends or you had to skimp on prom night (but the candle and floral arrangement on the table at McDonald's made it seem *just like* a fancy restaurant). Besides, if things got really tight, you could always play on your parents' sympathy. Maybe the conversation went something like this:

YOU: Mom, Dad, could I have a few bucks? Some friends and me want to go—

THEM: That's "Some friends and *I*."

YOU: Yeah, whatever. Some friends and *I* want to go out to eat after the game.

THEM: Why don't you spend your *own* cash for that? We aren't made of money, you know. It doesn't grow on trees. If all of your friends jumped off a cliff, would you?. . . Oh, wait, we got mixed up; we'll use that one for something else.

YOU: (*Whining.*) I never have enough money for anything.

THEM: (*Sarcastically.*) We feel *sooo* sorry for you. You are *sooo* underprivileged.

When you're on your own, the whole money thing changes. It gets worse. Money is harder to find and harder to keep. Everything costs more—because you're paying for it. But don't worry. With a little planning, diligence and self-deprivation on your part, and with a few practical and helpful tips on our part, you'll be able to afford everything you need. And occasionally, just occasionally, you'll even be able to afford a few nonessential luxuries (like getting your dinner super-sized for an extra 39 cents).

What You've Cost So Far

It has been estimated that middle-income families spend between $150,000 and $200,000 to raise a child from birth to age 17.

The Ups & Downs and Ins & Outs of Money Management

When it comes to managing your money, all you need to know and remember are four simple directions: in, out, up, down. Here's how those four simple directions relate to managing your finances when you are living on your own:

When your *outgo* exceeds your *income*,

then your *upkeep* will be your *downfall.*

We can even make it simpler than that: Don't spend more than you make.

Would You Pay $1,259 for a Combo Meal?

If you spend more than you make, you'll be getting deeper in debt each day. Suppose that each day you spend just $3.45 (the cost of a #3 combo meal without the supersize) more than you earn. That adds up to a little more than $100 a month. By the end of one year, you'll be in the hole $1,259. Now, that's a whopper of a debt for a hamburger.

Put a Budget Belt Around Your Waste

Without a budget, you'll have a difficult time determining whether the cost of your lifestyle is exceeding your income. Until now, you probably didn't need a budget. Most of your expenses were subsidized under the parental provision plan. Once you are on your own, however, your parents pay for less and less. (Read that last sentence to mean: "Once you are on your own, however, *you pay* for more and more.")

A budget is a simple way of figuring out what you can afford. It let's you know how much of your revenue is committed to the essentials that you have to pay for, and anything left over can be allocated for other things at your discretion. Budgeting is a simple process that begins with listing your income and your expenses.

Column A: Your Income
Make a list of your monthly income. This may not take very long. If you have odd jobs that don't pay regularly, then do your best to estimate the monthly average. Be realistic. Sure, Aunt Isabel used to send you $20 on your birthday every year, but do you really expect that to continue after high school? (And by the way, you must be really desperate if you are counting that $20, be-cause it only counts for $1.66 of monthly income when spread out over the whole year.)

Column B: Your Expenses
We bet this list will be a lot longer. What do you have to pay for? Write the amount down for your monthly expenses. Some will always be the same (such as car payments), so that will be easy. Others vary each month, depending upon your mood, your appetite and your car's mileage. So for expenses such as food, clothes and gasoline, you may want to talk to someone

who has been independent for a while to help you make a reasonable estimate. You might have to adjust your estimates after a few months (after you have some real-life experience with the bills).

Don't forget about expenses that don't get paid every month (such as car insurance). For these bills, you might only make two payments a year. Break these expenses down on a monthly basis. Maybe you pay college tuition at the beginning of each semester, but what is that amount per month? And don't just be thinking about you, you, you. What about planning for the charitable contributions that you will (or should) be making.

Be honest with yourself. If all of the employees at Starbucks know you as the "double, tall, vanilla latte with skim milk, heated to 175 degrees" customer, then estimate a lot more than just $15 a month for your food-and-snacks budget.

The Moment of Truth: Subtract the Total of Column B from the Total of Column A

If all goes well, the total on Column A will be more than the total on Column B. If it is, then congratulations.

1. *You have extra spending money each month.* Disburse the excess among the expense categories on Column B to give you a little

extra "fudge" factor (figuratively or literally, depending upon your cravings). Or put a new entry on Column B for something like "Getting Wild and Crazy," and then each month you can decide how to spend that extra $4.17. But before you actually spend any of that excess, read number 2.

2. *You are the first person in history who is unintentionally living within your means.* You must have made a mistake. Go back and check your figures. Did you include *all* of your expenses? (Your friends and family may not be too happy when they get no Christmas gifts from you. It will sound pretty lame for you to blame "budgetary design miscalculations.")

It is more likely that your expenses (Column B) will exceed your income (Column A). Join the club. Now you've got to get financially creative in order to make the amounts equal each other. You have two choices:

1. *Make more income.* Wow, there is something you never thought of before. Don't spend too much time here. If there were

something you could easily do to make more money, you'd probably already be doing it.

2. *Cut back on some of your expenses.* This is painful, but it is probably the only option for you. Maybe the first thing to go will be the $90 monthly expense for the daily double, tall, vanilla latte with skim milk, heated to 175 degrees.

Using a Budget Is Different from *Having* a Budget

Lots of people *have* a budget. Few people *use* one. After you create your budget, then you have to live within its parameters. Sometimes that's fun, and sometimes it's not. If you have allocated $40 a month for clothes and you only spend $30 in October, then you've got $50 to spend in November. On the other hand, if you have budgeted only a measly $25 a month for car repairs, then a new radiator cap could throw your budget out of whack.

If you are over in one account, you'll have to stay under in another. So don't be so quick to spend that extra $10 of clothes money from October. You won't look good wearing a radiator cap, but it will work better then stuffing a sweater vest in the radiator hole.

Paper or Plastic?

The supermarket isn't the only place where the question "Paper or plastic?" applies. It is a key consideration once you are in charge of handling your own finances. Should you use paper (cash, checks or a debit card) or plastic (credit cards)? Each system has its own advantages and drawbacks, but we think a checking account is the best choice if you are using a budget (notice we said *using* a budget).

Cash

If you are spending cash, it is hard to keep track of where it goes. To stay on a budget, at the beginning of each month you could put the cash for each expense item into separate envelopes. For example, if you're planning on spending $50 each month for gas, you put $50 in the envelope for gas and keep it in the glove compartment of your car. When you use up the money in the envelope, you stop buying gas for the month. (Just hope you aren't on the interstate 200 miles from home when your gas tank and your gas envelope simultaneously go empty.)

Credit Cards

Credit cards have the convenience of giving you buying power without your having to carry a wad of cash in your pocket. They also have the advantage of giving you a written record (the receipt and your monthly statement) for where your money went. This makes budgeting much easier and more accurate.

The disadvantage of credit cards is their illusion that you have more money than your budget may allow. When store clerks accept your credit card, they will never ask, "Are you sure this expenditure is within the parameters of your budgetary constraints?" You've got to keep track of your expenditures during the month so that you won't be surprised (and your budget won't be obliterated) when the bill comes the next month.

Credit card companies *love* college students. Not "love" as in a "have affection for" kind of way, but "love" as in a "make a lot of money off of" kind of way. Most college students, not having read this book, don't have the discipline to control their spending. The credit card companies can be pretty sure that college students will run their card balance to the credit limit and then get stuck paying double-digit interest (and late payment penalty fees) for years to come.

So be prepared for mass mailings of credit card offers. You'll get them all: the general ones (Visa, MasterCard, Discover Card) and the specialty ones (gasoline companies, department stores, electronic retailers).

We suggest that you pick one with a low limit—for

emergencies only—and pay it off each month without fail. Now here's the really important part: *Throw all of the other solicitations away.* After you start your own company, then you can have two: one for personal use and another for business. But for now, one is enough.

Don't borrow money from anyone who is anxious to loan it to you.

Checking Account

Once you are on your own, a checking account is a necessity. It is the safest way to hold your money (in the bank instead of your wallet), and it gives you an immediate record of what you spend your money on (assuming that you make a notation in the checkbook ledger every time you write a check). Of course, the total in your ledger won't be reliable unless you follow a few rules:

- *Write it down right away.* Take the extra 17 seconds to write the check number, payee, description and amount in the ledger when you write the check. You won't remember this information later in the evening after you eat dinner and fall asleep watching the syndicated rerun of *Friends*.

- *Reconcile your checkbook ledger each month.* This just means checking your ledger total against the total on your monthly bank statement or online report. DO NOT JUST CHANGE THE TOTAL IN YOUR CHECKBOOK LEDGER TO MATCH THE BANK'S RECORDS. You have to subtract from the bank statement or online total any outstanding checks—checks that haven't gone through the bank yet.

- *Watch those debit cards.* These cards are like charge cards, except that when the card is swiped, the money is immediately swiped from your checking account. There is nothing wrong with using them, but you need to remember to write the amount of the charge in your checkbook ledger. These cards are a relatively painless way to spend money. That's the problem with them.

Affording College: It Takes Money to Make Money

Your biggest expense over the next few years is going to be college. As we discussed in chapter 2, there are a lot of reasons to go to college. But strictly from a financial standpoint, a college education is a wise investment because most college graduates make much more money during their working lives than those without college degrees.

Cost: Last but Not Least

When you are choosing which college or university to attend, the cost is not the *least* important factor, but it should be the *last* factor you consider. What we mean is that your decision should first be made without considering the cost. Decide which particular college or university is best for you based on the many nonfinancial factors mentioned in chapter 2. (Do you want a small college or a large university? Which school has the best program for the major you are interested in? Christian or secular? Private or public? Liberal arts or research and technology?)

After you have decided which kind of institution will best equip you for the kind of person you want to be and for the career you're interested in, *then* look at the cost.

If your parents get a hold of this book, they'll probably rip out this section. They'll say that college expenses are a major part of the decision process. We agree, but we think there isn't just one big decision. There are two separate decisions.

Decision 1

Which is the best college or institution for
you (ignoring financial considerations)?

After you have the answer to Decision 1, then you
move to the second stage:

Decision 2

How can you make the financial arrangements for the school you have selected?

Paying Less Than the Cost

Very few college students pay the full amount of what
their college education costs. It is not uncommon for
80 to 90 percent of the student population to be on
some form of assistance. Here are a few of the financial
aid opportunities that may be available to you at the
institution of your choice:

- *Academic Scholarships.* Many schools will provide
  a scholarship to be used toward tuition if your
  GPA and SAT or ACT scores are high enough.
  The brainiacs can get a full-ride scholarship,

but even the less-than-genius types can receive a major discount—scholarships unrelated to financial need.

- *Athletic Scholarships.* Sports programs play a major role in college life. Each school's reputation and publicity is tied into the success of its sports teams. If you are really good at running or jumping or throwing, the school may pay to get you on its team.

- *Other Scholarships.* If you're in the middle of the pack academically and athletically, don't despair. There are a lot of scholarships awarded for other criteria. Maybe your college has a scholarship for mediocre students with blond hair who major in kinesiology. You got the mediocre part covered, and a stop at the drugstore can take care of the blond hair, and you're sure you'll want to major in kinesiology (as soon as someone explains what it is).

- *Grants.* Federal and state grants (money that you don't have to pay back) are available on the basis of financial need.

- *Loans.* Loans from the federal and state governments and from the school may be available. These loans have to be paid, but they are usually at low interest or no interest. The repayment schedule usually begins after graduation (which is an incentive for you to go to work after college).

- *Work Study*. Where do you think the college gets its cheap labor force? Someone has to spread the fertilizer on the grass and dish out the green beans in the dining commons (usually these are separate jobs).

Here's the point of all of this: There are lots of ways to accomplish the financing of your college education. Contact the financial aid office, and investigate all of the options. It will be the best investment you ever make.

Moving On

All the money in the world won't do you much good if you are nailed shut in a pine box buried six feet under and pushing up daisies. You probably haven't had to think about your health very often. Until this point in your life, you probably haven't had to. Your mother took care of that (with the vitamin C at breakfast and broccoli at dinner). But once you are on your own, you are responsible for your own health. That could be a scary thought, so the next chapter will help you figure out how to stay alive (and we won't mention broccoli once).

Healthy Choices

Preparing Your Body to Last a Lifetime

That "freshman 15" thing is no joke. It really happens.

JANICE O., AGE 20

If you don't already know it, we've got news for you: You aren't going to live forever. Well, at least your *body* isn't. Your *soul*—the spiritual part of you—is going to live forever (more about that in chapter 11). But your body is an entirely different matter.

Everything about your body is finite. There are limitations. If you take care of your body, it should serve you well for 70, 80, even 90 years (and if you make it to your 100th birthday, you might get mentioned on the local news, but you'll probably be sleeping through the broadcast).

There are no guarantees, of course, that you won't contract a life-threatening disease or get hit by a train. Sometimes things happen, and we don't know the reason. But there is plenty you can do to care for the amazing physical body God has given you.

Now Is the Time for Health

Up until now you've been blessed with a young and strong body. You've been able to eat junk food, dive into mosh pits and basically sit around without any serious damage to your system. When you participate in a strenuous outdoor activity, such as hiking, water-skiing or bowling, you wake up the next morning without feeling stiff (believe us, that won't always be the case).

It's a remarkable machine, your body. About the only downside it has experienced is the presence of acne—and that's fading quickly. So you'd better enjoy your strong and healthy body while you still can. And while you're at it, why not start planning for the rest of your life right now?

Choose to steer clear of risky behavior and destructive habits. That doesn't mean you have to settle for a boring, low-key life. We're not asking you to play it *safe*. We're asking you to play it *smart*. All the dreams and desires in the world won't mean a thing if you abuse your body. What good is standing on top of the world if you're on your last leg? "Don't you realize that all of you together are the temple of God and that the Spirit of God lives in you?" (1 Corinthians 3:16).

Take care of yourself. From the standpoint of wear and tear, these are the best days your body will ever have. There will never be a better time to begin the habits of healthy living.

It's like starting a savings account. If you put 20 bucks a week into savings now, you'll have a comfortable retirement. If you wait until you retire to start saving, it won't help you a bit. The same goes for your body. If you begin now to establish a lifetime of health, you'll enjoy the dividends of health for a lifetime.

Why Bring It Up Now?

Why deal with health issues now? Can't it wait until after you're through school and in the routine of a job and eventually a family? No, this can't wait. Here are two reasons:

1. The *bad* habits you start now will *hinder* you for the rest of your life.
2. The *good* habits you start now will *help* you for the rest of your life.

You more or less fall into bad habits without realizing it. They sneak up on you in small ways and become a part of your routine over time. Some bad habits are annoying but harmless:

- Uncle Charlie's habit of sucking through his teeth in a futile attempt to dislodge particles of food that have been there since last Christmas
- Cousin Billy's habit of hocking up lugies and then swallowing them
- Your habit of never making your bed (unlike Uncle Charlie's and Cousin Billy's bad habits, your habit annoys only one person—your mom)

Other habits are harmless most of the time but have the potential to get you into trouble:

- Grandpa's habit of backing up in traffic without looking
- Your neighbor's habit of letting his dog poop on your lawn
- Your habit of always being 10 minutes late

Then there are those habits that seem harmless enough at first and don't seem to have any immediate consequences. However, over time, there is an absolute certainty that any one of these habits will lead to serious consequences and negative health issues.

Eating

Research has proven that if you ingest too much fat, too many calories and too much cholesterol into your system, you will do damage to your body in the long haul. One of the advantages you have now is a resilient body. You can eat all the burgers you want and still maintain your weight and healthy glow.

Here are some of the ways your eating habits will get you in the end (sorry) unless you develop betters ones *now*.

Eating the Wrong Things. There's an old saying that

goes, "You are what you eat." If that were true, many Americans would look like a pizza or a French fry (come to think of it, many of them do). Actually, the truth in that statement is that your health—and to a large extent your appearance—is directly related to the foods you eat.

Hear us now, believe us later. If you continue to eat with abandon through your prime years, we guarantee that your waistline (if you're a guy) or hips (if you're a girl) will have a larger circumference than they do now. And that's just on the *outside*. Only God (and eventually your doctor) knows what's going on in the *inside*.

> **Gluttony—literally *excess eating*—is listed in classical literature as one of the Seven Deadly Sins. The Bible pretty much puts it in the same category as drunkenness (see Proverbs 23:20-21).**

Eating Too Much. The biggest eating problem most Americans have—and this includes most people your age—is that they eat too much. Unless you're an athlete in serious training, or you are blessed with the metabolism of a hummingbird, you probably don't need to eat as much as you do. Here are some guidelines for those who overachieve in the eating arena:

- Don't eat until you're stuffed; eat until you're full.
- Don't go back for seconds—or thirds.
- Skip dessert unless it's your birthday.
- Don't eat snacks before you go to bed.
- Keep healthy snacks in your room to munch on when you're hungry during the day.

Not Eating Enough. Skipping meals because you're too busy or starving yourself because you suddenly think you're overweight is really dumb—and destructive. Eating disorders among kids have been well publicized, and they are serious matters that require professional help. But you don't have to be suffering from anorexia or bulimia to do damage to your body. Going on crash diets is never a good idea, and besides, you always gain back the weight.

Smoking

According to the United States Department of Health and Human Services, smoking is the leading preventable cause of death in the United States.[1] That's the good news—that the health problems caused by smoking are *preventable.* The other bit of good news is that the number of students who smoke is declining.[2]

Still, the number of young people who smoke

ranges between 9 percent of eighth-grade students and 25 percent of twelfth-grade students.[3] That's a shame, mainly because of those special physical qualities and mysterious allure that smoking produces:

- Yellow teeth and fingers
- Bad breath
- Pale, crinkly skin
- A delightful cough
- Reduced lung capacity
- Reduced life expectancy

Smoke at Home

What do you do if someone in your family smokes, especially one or both of your parents? Treat them with love and respect, but definitely voice your concerns for their health (not to mention yours). Tell them that no matter how long they've smoked, it's never too late to quit. The health benefits of quitting abound, regardless of age.

Drinking

Drinking is a pretty controversial subject. Social drinking is acceptable in most circles, including some religious ones (frankly, the Bible doesn't prohibit drinking;

it just instructs us not to get drunk—see Ephesians 5:18). On the other hand, some people believe that it's never right to drink because of where it can lead you.

We want to strike a little balance by suggesting two things:

1. If you're underage, never drink. Don't even try.
2. Just because you're able to drink, don't think you have to. Don't buckle under peer pressure (there's plenty of it, no matter how old you are).

Even if you think you can handle alcohol, you need to be aware that everyone who ends up with a drinking problem once thought he or she could handle it. And it doesn't take a long time to go from having no problem to having a serious one.

The fact of the matter is that drinking is a real problem among college-aged people. Here's some sobering information from *College Clues for the Clueless:*

- Student drinking is the number one health problem on college campuses today.
- Alcohol is a "factor" in 41 percent of all academic problems.

· Ninety percent of rapes occur while either the rapist or the victim is under the influence of alcohol.

· If there's a crime on campus, alcohol is usually involved.[4]

Taking Drugs

Unfortunately, drugs and college students seem to go together. Ever since Professor Timothy Leary (ask your parents about him, right after you ask them about Euell Gibbons) suggested that America's youth "tune in, turn on, drop out" through mind-altering drugs, an alarming number of students have done just that.

Why do students turn to drugs? Conventional wisdom suggests that any one of the following anxieties can contribute to drug use: personal pressure, insecurity, loneliness and the need to belong.

Good Habits, Good Results

We've talked enough about bad habits. Now it's time to focus on good habits. But before we get to our list of the Top 3 constructive health habits, we want to make sure you understand something. Let's put it in the form of a *Bruce & Stan Truism*:

Your good habits will be much more effective if you eliminate your bad habits.

We're not saying that you need to get rid of every bad habit before you can start good habits (if that were the case, we'd all be in trouble). What we are saying is that where your body is concerned, the good stuff you put in will be much more effective if you stop putting bad stuff in.

Let's go through some basic good health habits. These aren't so difficult.

Health Habit 1: Eating Right

Earlier in this chapter we encouraged you to play it *smart*. This is especially true when it comes to eating for healthy results. We aren't experts in this field, but there are plenty of people who are. We found Cheryl Townsley and her book *Food Smart!* Cheryl recommends that you avoid these foods: caffeine, alcohol, foods with preservatives or additives, high-sodium products, MSG, refined sugar, white flour, margarine, white rice, carbonated beverages and smoked foods.[5]

How to Avoid the Freshman 15

The famous "freshman 15" describes what happens when students leave home for college and start eating like Homer Simpson and, before they know it, they begin to look like Homer Simpson.

It's easy to avoid gaining those 15 extra pounds. Most college dining commons have improved their selections tremendously, adding healthy foods and juices to the menu. All you have to do is eat smart, avoiding such waistline expanders as junk-food snacks and late-night burger binges. Stock your own healthy snacks for those times when you do get the munchies.

Health Habit 2: Exercising

In her excellent book *Greater Health God's Way*, Stormie Omartian says that "exercise is just as important in weight loss as proper diet."[6] Eating healthily will help you, but when you combine your good eating habits with a regular exercise routine, you'll maintain or even lose weight while keeping a fit appearance.

When we say "exercise," we don't mean fanatical, endorphin-popping, budget-breaking exercise that takes hours of time and hundreds of dollars. We're talking about

- Walking, jogging or running
- Bicycling
- Sensible weight training
- Team sports (such as basketball, volleyball and tennis)

The important thing is to choose something you enjoy and then follow Nike's advice: *Just do it!*

Health Habit 3: Sleeping

Sleep is very underrated as a factor in health. The truth is that your body—including your brain—repairs and rebuilds itself during sleep. And the truth is also that when you get on out your own, you feel like you never want to sleep! There are so many new experiences, so many things to do, so many new people to meet. And then when you think you've done everything you possibly can in a 24-hour period, you realize that you have to study. So you pull an all-nighter. And after several weeks of this crazy routine, you wonder why you're feeling lousy or even down-right sick.

Now we're not going to suggest that you get eight hours of sleep every night. That's too much to ask. But you can do better than the four or five hours that you might be getting now.

Managing Stress: It's All in Your Mind

Too many commitments cause stress, and stress causes your body to do strange things. Your heart races, your blood pressure rises, your muscles tighten, your appetite increases or decreases, and often your mood changes. Not good. You need a way to manage stress.

Just like everything else in this chapter, managing stress is a matter of bringing balance to your life and using your head. You don't need to make an appointment with a medical doctor or a psychologist (unless you're demonstrating some serious symptoms) in order to reduce your stress. Just use some common sense. Hey, if you'd have thought about it long enough, you could have come up with these seven stress-busters yourself:

- Eat healthy foods
- Exercise regularly
- Get enough sleep
- Get organized
- Learn to say no
- Talk it out
- Pray

While you won't be able to eliminate your stress—no one ever has—you can successfully manage it. And the result will be a healthier, happier life.

Moving On

In this and the preceding chapters, we have been talking about the new you: new address, new friends, new experiences, new adventures.

But there is a part of the old you that still lingers behind and shouldn't be forgotten. We're talking about your family. You remember them—those parents and siblings with whom you have been living for 18 years. Even though you will be off to bigger and better things, they will still play a big part in your life after high school. The dynamics of those relationships, however, will never be the same.

In chapter 9, we'll give you a little insight about how those relationships will change so that you can be prepared for it before it happens.

Family Ties

Out of Sight, but Not Forgotten

It's only after you leave home that you really start to appreciate everything your parents did for you. It's never too late to tell them.

MARK A., AGE 23

When you reach that senior year in high school, you are feeling pretty secure. You've got the high-school-studying thing down pat (which doesn't necessarily mean that you are studying; it may mean that you know how to get by without studying). You've mastered the art of making friends (and knowing what kind of people you should avoid) on campus.

By the spring semester of your senior year, you are even learning how to communicate with your parents and understand them. Well, "understanding" may be a bit of a stretch; let's just accept the fact that you are communicating with them much better than you did a couple of years before. Your life has a nice, tranquil feel to it.

Then, in less time than it takes to unzip your rented graduation robe, there will be some drastic changes. Not everything changes. Some things stay the same. If you're going to college, you'll still have to contend with studying (and your college classes may be very similar to your old high-school classes; even those desk-and-chair combos are the same size). And making friends and avoiding enemies isn't going to be all that much different either.

The dramatic changes in your life are going to happen in your home. Oh, your mom and dad will still be your parents, and your brothers and sisters will still be your siblings, but the dynamics of your relationships will change, and they will never, ever go back to the way they were before.

How to Say Good-Bye

Your parents have survived your progression from diapers to diploma. During that time it was *you* who made most of the changes. Now, all of a sudden, it's your parents who will have to make the most dramatic adjustments. Sure, you will continue to change a little bit at a time as you make the transition into adulthood, but your parents will have to go through a major role change. They have spent almost two decades as "hands-on managers." After your graduation from high school, their positions will change drastically to that of "outside consultants."

Your Perspective
When you begin life out on your own, whether as a college student or as a working adult, you will be leading a relatively independent life.

- You will expect that rules be replaced by your own emphasis on personal responsibility.
- You will view freedom as a necessary component

of your maturing process.

- You will consider that your personal independence overshadows any vestiges of obligation or accountability to your parents.
- You will resent continued intrusion and meddling in your life by your parents.

These are all natural, reasonable feelings on your part. But they are completely opposite from your parents' perspective.

Your Parents' Perspective

You might think of yourself as an adult, but your parents have all those memories of you being a goofy, irresponsible kid. When you start to assert your independence and take offense when they impose restrictions, you're likely to hear comments such as these:

- "You are still just a kid."
- "Is this the thanks we get for all our slaving and sacrifice?"
- And the infamous "As long as you are living in our house, you'll play by our rules."

These are all natural, reasonable and understandable feelings for your parents to have. (Remember, they heard the same things from *their parents*. It is kind of a 30-year déjà vu thing.)

Patience Required

Particularly if you are the oldest child, your parents are going to be struggling to learn their new roles in life. They are no longer wardens or even coaches. When you are out and on your own, they are sort of like concierges—they are standing by, anxious to help and advise you, but only if you come to them with questions.

You can help your parents through this difficult transition if you are sensitive to the transformation they must make.

- *They're learning to check in with you instead of checking up on you.* They will be curious about what is going on in your life. Give them the benefit of the doubt. Assume that their inquiries are made from their heartfelt curiosity and are not intended to be judgmental.
- *They're learning to listen instead of lecture.* For 18 years or so, they were doing the talking, and you were (supposed to be) doing the listening. But after you graduate from high school, they must flip-flop and suddenly be quick to listen and slow to speak. They are anxious to develop

an adult-to-adult relationship with you that fosters communication.

- *They're learning to give advice only when asked.* Your parents don't want you to make the same mistakes that they made, so they are anxious to bless you with their sage wisdom and knowledge. But be patient. Sooner or later they will learn that you will be much more receptive to their advice when you decide to ask for it. (Periodically, just for the fun of it, ask your parents a "What do you think I should do?" question. They will feel *so* fulfilled.)

- *They're learning to ask questions for the sake of praying, not for prying.* All of the sudden your parents have to abandon the litany of the "who, what, when" cross-examination techniques they developed when you were in high school. They know they are more likely to get information out of you now if they phrase their questions in a more generic form, such as, "How should we pray for you?"

- *They're learning to let you live under their roof but not under their thumb.* If you are living away from home, the hardest adjustment will be on those weekends, holidays and vacations when you return home. Your parents will have memories and recollections of the rules that were in place during high school, but you will be living in a relatively unrestricted environment. Maybe your parents won't feel the need to impose the old "rules of the house" if you are quick to display courtesy and respect by letting them know what you will be doing and where you will be going.

Your parents' love for you won't diminish when you become an adult and leave home, but the way in which they interact with you will be drastically different. There is a delicate art to this transition: mothering without monitoring, loving without leading and interacting without intruding. Your parents understand the distinctions, but it may take them a while to make the transformation. Give them a little slack.

Keep Your Parents in the Loop

Despite all of the jokes about gaining an extra bedroom, your parents are going to be sad when you leave home. After all, they stuck by you when you were going through those rebellious, snotty teenage years. Now, just when you're becoming an adult and your parents are enjoying your friendship at that level, you're moving out. How rude!

It will be hard on your parents because they will feel as if they were losing a friend. They will feel out of the loop because they don't know what is going on in your life. But you can solve that problem with these four simple suggestions:

1. *Get a digital camera.* Take pictures of your new friends and your activities and e-mail them to your parents. Hey, you're parents may even pay for the camera as an incentive to get the pictures.

2. *Send them a copy of your college newspaper.* You won't read everything in the paper, but your parents will. They will be able to live your college life vicariously through each issue.

3. *Send them a copy of your class schedule.* You don't have a difficult time getting a mental picture of where your parents are because you are totally familiar with their jobs and their schedules. But if you are away at college, they won't know anything about your daily schedule unless you tell them.

4. *Invite them to come and visit you.* They could

go overboard with this, so you will have to use caution. If you leave for your freshman year of college on September 1, they'll be ready to come for a visit by September 6. We think this is a little too soon (and we know that you'll think it is *way* too soon). But by the end of October, you will be ready, and your parents will be eager to visit. By then you will have made some friends, and you're parents probably won't deny your request to take you all out to dinner at a nice restaurant.

If you're living in an apartment or a dorm in your hometown, the same rule applies. They will be glad to spend time with you and your friends because they will be interested in getting an update on what's happening in your life.

Give Your Parents a Clue

Your parents will want to stay involved in your life, and they'll want to help out and do nice things for you. (Absence makes the heart grow fonder, and all that mush.) But your parents may need a few suggestions of what they can send you. So you don't get stuck with a lot of stuff that you don't want (like socks and vitamins), give them ideas of what you do want:

- *Your hometown newspaper.* Tell your parents that you don't care if the city council approves the zoning for the waste disposal plant, but you *do* care about your favorite high-school teams and activities.
- *Your magazine subscriptions.* Perhaps your parents won't notice that the postage to send them to you is more than the full cover price of the magazines.
- *Packages filled with goodies.* Here you may want to specify that your definition of "goodies" includes Oreos and M&Ms but excludes socks and vitamins.

Don't Let This Happen to You

A son who was away at college wrote this cryptic e-mail message to his father in the hope that he would get a little spending money:

No fun. No mon. Your son.

The father's prompt reply was equally succinct:

Too bad. So sad. Your dad.

If you're going to ask for money, don't be as crass and blatant as the son in this frequently told story. At least disguise your request by telling your folks a little about what is happening in your life.

Siblings at Home

As tough as it will be for your parents when you leave home, it could be worse on any younger brothers or sisters whom you leave behind. You have been their big brother or big sister for their entire lives. They have looked up to you (figuratively and literally). Oh, sure, they might have acted like little pests for a while, but that is only because they were trying to get your attention.

Don't forget to be considerate about the feelings of your younger siblings when you go away to college or move out on your own. They may possibly feel forgotten or unloved. After all, your parents will be making quite a fuss over you. *You* will be getting all of the attention; *you* are the one who is taking the extra television set. It's all you, you, you.

With a little planning, you can make the transition

a little less painful for your younger siblings. Take the time to do these things:

- Send them e-mails on a regular basis.
- If you're away at college, send them a shirt or cap with your college logo.
- Come home for their birthdays.
- Invite them to stay with you for a day or two.

A little kindness now could reap big dividends in the future. Sixty years from now you'll be glad that you have younger siblings. Maybe they will come to visit you in the nursing home.

Back Home

Sooner or later, after you have been away for several months, you will return home for the first time. Maybe it will be over the Thanksgiving holiday. Maybe it will be for Christmas vacation. Whenever that first time arrives, as you walk through the door of your house, it will be like stepping into Bizarre-O-World.

It won't seem strange at first. There will be the typical greeting rituals. Your mom will kiss you, your dad will hug you, your dog will sniff you, and your little brother will sniff you, too. Then you will throw your trash bag full of dirty clothes into the laundry room and move to your room to make a few phone calls to friends you haven't seen for a while.

There! Right at that point, you notice a funny look on your parents' faces. But in ignorant bliss, you make the calls. Another contorted expression appears on their faces when you tell them that you are going out to dinner with your friends. Your mother starts whimpering like an injured squirrel. You think to yourself, *Do they* really *think that I'm going to spend all of my free time with them?* Well, we're here to tell you, "Yes, they do!"

Once you realize that you and your parents have opposite expectations, it will be easier for you to negotiate a treaty for peaceful coexistence.

Stepping Back in Time

When you lived at home in the "old days," before you moved away, you were still living under the house rules imposed on you by your parents. One of the reasons you left home may have been to get away from some of those rules. And whether you objected to the rules or not, you won't be living under anything close to the same rules in a college dorm or in your own apartment.

But your parents still remember those rules, and they still consider them to apply to you when you're back home (even if the visit is for a few days). And they will just assume that you remember all of the rules, so they won't review them with you ahead of time.

Avoiding Inevitable Conflicts

When you are back home, you will do everyone a favor if you go overboard in sharing your plans with your parents. Let them know where you are going and who will be with you. If you go out for a night of activities, tell them when you plan to be home. Let them know whether you plan to eat at home with the family or whether you will have dinner with someone else. We know this may seem a bit extreme, but when you think about it, this is all a matter of courteous communication.

Moving On

Moving out on your own is one of the fun aspects about becoming an adult. Another feature of adulthood, less fun at times, is working a job. In the next chapter, we will look at the wonderful world of work that awaits you.

Jobs and Careers

So What Are You Going to Do?

I knew I wanted to serve the Lord and follow His will, but I couldn't decide between majoring in business or in religious studies (to be a youth pastor). Then a friend told me, "We've got a lot of youth pastors, but we could sure use some more Christian business-men." Then I knew exactly what the Lord wanted me to do.

JON C., AGE 24

If you could take only one thing away from this book, here is what we hope it is:

Live life on purpose, because there's a purpose for your life.

You're not here by accident. There's a reason for your existence. Your life and what you do really do matter.

Living Your Life in Three Tenses

No matter where you are in life, you will always be living your life in three tenses. Here's what we mean:

- You are the product of your *past*, which prepared you for what you are doing now.
- You are experiencing life in the *present* in a very dynamic way as you learn from and interact with others.
- You are hopeful and preparing for the *future*, which includes people you haven't met and experiences you haven't had.

The Antidote for Fear and the Alternative to Pressure

We don't mean to make you nervous about your life right now. We're not saying that you've got to get out there in the real world and make your mark by next week. You're in a period of preparation, and that's going to take a few years.

On the other hand, maybe it's time for you to get out of the nest, which could be your parents' home or another comfortable, safe place, such as school. Or you could be working in a so-so job that you don't want to do forever. The fact of the matter is that you're too comfortable and too dependent on others. You might be afraid of what could go wrong if you step out in an attempt to find your place and make your mark in this world.

The Antidote for Fear Is Trust

All of us fear the future to some degree. It's only natural. But you can't let your fear paralyze you. If you want to get things done and find your place, you have to move on. But you're nervous and afraid. What should you do?

The only antidote to fear that we have found is *trust*. You have to trust that there will be opportunities for you and your skills. You have to trust other people to respond favorably to your talents and desires. Most of all—since the doors of opportunity sometimes close and people can and will let you down—you have to trust God.

That's not as difficult as it seems. What you have to do is keep in constant communication with Him by allowing Him to talk to you through His Word as you talk to Him through prayer. You will be amazed how God will guide you to His plans one step at a time.

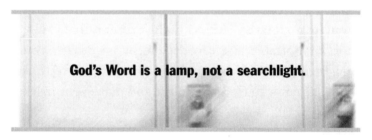

God's Word is a lamp, not a searchlight.

If you are like us, you are anxious to know everything about your future. But God knows better. He knows, for example, that if you did know everything, you would either take your eyes off Him or run scared. That's why the Bible describes itself as a lamp for your feet and a light for your path (see Psalm 119:105). God will give you just enough illumination for your next step, not for the rest of your life.

The Alternative to Pressure Is a Plan

As you step out in faith and find your place in this world, you're going to feel pressure:

- Pressure to find the right job or career.
- Pressure to compete once you're in that job or career.
- Pressure that you'll make the wrong choice.

That's why a plan is so important. If you don't have a plan to get you *somewhere*, you'll end up going *nowhere*. To our way of thinking, the path to your plan involves *work*.

Work Matters

Here's the deal. The next few years are going to be the optimum time for you to decide what you want to *do*—which is closely tied to whom you want to *be*. Now, we're not saying that you need to belabor your decision to work part-time at the Gap to pay for books (although your jobs in college can give you a clue about what your long-term aspirations might be). And that's not to say there won't be opportunities for you to change gears later in life—there are 40-year-old housewives who return to school and to the work force after spending years at home. But the longer you wait, the harder it can be.

If you're heading to college, you have some time. No one is pushing you to chisel out your career path in stone—yet. On the other hand, if you have opted to skip college and to work right out of high school, your situation is a little more delicate. Working full-time pulling down $10 an hour is okay—as long as you're living at home or with three roommates. But sometime in the next few years, you're going to have to figure out what you want to do for the foreseeable future, if not for the rest of your life.

The Privilege of Work

Work is a blessing from God—ideally. We are very aware that work can discourage and dehumanize people. More than half of the world's population live in poverty, unable to work at a level that gives them dignity, let alone provides for their families. Many lack even the most basic necessities.

If this causes you to stop and think, and perhaps even feel a little guilty, that's okay. Later in the chapter we're going to give you some ideas as to how you can do something to help others in need.

For now, let's concentrate on you, because you

won't help anyone by sitting around feeling sorry for the world or feeling guilty for living in the most prosperous society on Earth. Yes, you are privileged. The very fact that you can read makes you privileged (according to UNESCO, there are more than 800 million illiterate adults in the world).[1] And the fact that you have the option to go to college makes you privileged.

Never mind what kind of income you will have in the future. The fact is that you have *opportunity* to work and to succeed. That alone makes you privileged. What you need to think about is what you are going to do with what you have. Because you are privileged, are you going to live responsibly before God and the world? Or are you going to squander your talents and resources because your priorities are in the wrong order?

> Much is required from those to whom much is given, and much more is required from those to whom much more is given (Luke 12:48).

Who Do You Want to Become?

You see, from where you are now, ready to begin to prepare for your future career, it's not a question of what you want to do. The question you need to be asking yourself is *Who do I want to become?*

Yes, you will *do* something. But who you want to become will influence what you will do (or at least it should). Don't get caught in the unfulfilling cycle of pursuing a career or a profession because it offers the most money or the most opportunity for advancement. There's nothing wrong with ambition (in fact, we encourage it), but your ambitions will be more productive and fulfilling if they're plugged in to a purpose for your life.

If you base your career ambitions on your purpose for life, you're going to stand out from the crowd. Many people pursue materialism as a motive for working, which is why many people are unhappy in their work.

Our experience is that regardless of the job, career or profession, the people who are happiest and most fulfilled are those whose work comes out of a sense of who they are and what they want to contribute to the world. Does this mean you need to aspire to be another Mother Teresa, who lived among the poor and the sick in Calcutta? Possibly, but not necessarily. The more probable scenario for you is that you will end up doing something very ordinary. But it won't be your work that defines you. Rather, you will define your work. And that's what will raise you and your work from the ordinary to the extraordinary.

What Are You Looking For?

Over the next few years, as you find what you want to do, you're going to have to choose how you will define your work. The story is often told of three bricklayers who were working side by side on a church construction project. When the first bricklayer was asked what he was going, he said, "I'm laying bricks. What does it look like I'm doing?" The second bricklayer responded, "I'm laying bricks for this wall, which will be an important part of this building." The third bricklayer replied, "I'm building a cathedral that's going to glorify God."

The choice is yours. Will you view your work as

- a *job* where you simply earn a paycheck,
- a *career* where you can climb the ladder, or
- a *mission* where you can make a difference in what you do?

Are You Available?

What you need to realize is that God can use you wherever you are, as long as you are available. The prophet Isaiah was available to God. When God asked, "Whom should I send as a messenger to my people?" Isaiah immediately responded, "Lord, I'll go! Send me" (Isaiah 6:7-8).

That doesn't mean that God is going to send you into the deepest, darkest jungles of Brazil—but it might. It doesn't necessarily mean that you will have to give up your job so that you can serve God full-time—but it might. And it doesn't necessarily mean that you won't have lots of money—but it might.

Being available to God, whether you are a student, an employee or an employer, means that you are willing to do whatever it takes and to do whatever He wants. And the chances are very good that God will want to use you right where you are to influence the people around you.

Vocation Versus Avocation

A *vocation* is a particular job, business, profession or trade. An *avocation* is something you do besides your job or profession. For most people, their hobbies—such as sailing or skiing—are their avocations. Can we issue you a challenge? Don't make your hobby your avocation. Think bigger. Make your avocation something that contributes to the betterment of others. And if you're really clever, you'll work your hobby into your avocation (for example, you could donate your time to teach people with disabilities how to ski).

The Money Factor

Before we discuss money, we want to clarify one thing: Money isn't evil. As the Bible says, "The love of money is at the root of all kinds of evil" (1 Timothy 6:10), but money isn't evil in itself.

People will do all sorts of nasty things in order to get money. We're guessing that isn't your problem. If you're like the rest of us, here's where you're vulnerable:

Those who love money will never have enough. How absurd to think that wealth brings true happiness! (Ecclesiastes 5:10).

It would be good to memorize that verse now. Following the Bible's advice will save you a lot of grief and stress in the future.

While money should not be the number one factor in your search for a career, it certainly needs to be considered. In fact, at the risk of sounding like we're contradicting ourselves, we advise you to learn as much as you can about money management (start by rereading chapter 7 in this book). Then, as you search for a career path, look for something that can best fulfill your life's purpose while adequately providing for your material needs. If God blesses you with more than you need, invest it wisely in places that pay both spiritual and material dividends.

How to Work for Your Master

Chances are that you have already had at least one job. Before you start your career, you will no doubt have more jobs. And because some—if not all—of these jobs will have nothing to do with your eventual career, you may have a tendency to treat them as mere necessities, not worthy of your absolute best.

As two guys who have worked with and employed plenty of high-school and college-aged people, we can tell you that the person who slacks off in a part-time job at Burger Time is not on the road to a stellar career in aerospace. Conversely, the person who works hard and honestly even in a low-paying job is more likely to succeed in his or her chosen career.

Do You Feel like a Slave?

The Bible is very specific on how to work for your employers (only it refers to them as your master—and to you as their slave). Read Ephesians 6:5-9, and you'll discover some principles that will energize you and glorify God, no matter what job you have or whom you employ. *Employees* are to serve their bosses sincerely, to work hard and "with enthusiasm, as though you were working for the Lord rather than for people" (Ephesians 6:7). Likewise, *employers* are to treat their employees right, with respect and fairness—because our ultimate Master treats us all fairly.

It *Is* Who You Know

You've heard the expression "It's not *what* you know but *who* you know that counts." Now don't get carried away with this, but at time you'll want to put this principle into practice—especially when it comes to pleasing your bosses.

Your attitude and willingness to take on new assignments, to go the extra mile and to take the initiative will get you noticed and promoted. Employers are looking for skilled and knowledgeable workers, but they would much rather have skilled and knowledgeable people who work with industry and integrity.

And if you really buy into the notion that God, your ultimate master, is watching you, then you just have to trust that He is going to open more doors of opportunity for those who honor Him by serving their earthly masters with sincerity, diligence and enthusiasm.

How to Get a Job and Keep a Job

We mentioned earlier that between us we have hired lots of people. Now we'd like to give you some advice, from our experience, on getting and keeping a job.

Getting a Job

A resume is great—and it may get you a job interview—but it's not going to get you a job. The job interview is the key. Here's how you handle it:

1. Be on time.
2. Dress appropriately (it's better to be too dressed up than too casual).
3. Be enthusiastic and responsive—but don't talk too much.
4. Do a little homework; find out something about the company you want to work for.
5. Ask questions about the company's philosophy or mission statement.
6. Don't bring up money—let them do it.
7. Never talk negatively about your former employers.
8. Thank your interviewer and send a follow-up thank-you letter.

9. Follow up by phone within a week if you haven't heard a response.

10. Pray hard.

Keeping a Job

Getting a job is just one part of the battle. Keeping a job you like is another matter. Here are our tips:

1. Be on time every day.
2. Dress appropriately (it's better to be too dressed up than too casual).
3. Be enthusiastic and responsive.
4. Learn all you can about the company and its customers.
5. Do your best to fulfill the company's mission statement.
6. Don't ask for a raise—let them offer (unless you haven't had a raise in a year or more, in which case it's appropriate to bring it up).
7. Never talk negatively about your boss or fellow employees.
8. Show appreciation to those you work for and work with as well as to those who work for you.
9. Offer to take an extra project.
10. Pray hard.

Moving On

Although we hope you have had some fun along the way, we have been talking about some rather serious stuff: your college education, your finances and your career. But each of these aspects of your life needs to be held in balance, and you can stay balanced only if you have the proper perspective on life.

In the next chapter, we're going to talk about perspective. Specifically, we'll consider how you view the world. We'll be asking how God fits into your worldview and how you see yourself fitting in.

God and Your Worldview

Can You See Forever?

Life in the world and living for yourself are painful.
Living for God brings hope and joy.

TIFFANY A., AGE 19

Until now, your life has been a matter of multiple choice. From now on, life will be more like an essay test.

Throughout your life, people have told you what to do and what to think. Much like a multiple-choice test, you've been making choices between options prescribed by someone else. Don't feel bad. Until now your body and your brain—in that order—have been in development. People who have been giving you advice—your teachers, your parents, McGruff the Crime Dog—have all thought that the only thing you could handle was multiple choice. Usually the answers were pretty clear, so you could successfully pass the various "tests" in your life and move on to the next level. No one really cared *how* or *why* you knew what you knew (as long as you weren't cheating). They just wanted to know *that* you knew.

Now that you're moving on and possibly moving out, this whole business of knowing is going to change. This is when the "essay test" of life begins. All of a sudden, *what* you believe and *why* are going to become important. You're going to be required to do some independent thinking.

Your Worldview Is Showing

Your *worldview* shapes what you believe and why. What

is a worldview? Simply put, your worldview is the framework or context in which you consider the world at large and your place in it. A worldview is a perspective on the significance and consequences of issues in all aspects of life, which affects your thinking and behavior. And everyone has one. Even the poor slob who says, "Hey, I don't need no stinkin' worldview; I do what I want, when I want," has a worldview (although it is not one we endorse).

We agree with David Noebel, who wrote what we think is the definitive book on worldview, *Understanding the Times*. Noebel writes:

> Every individual bases his thoughts, decisions, and actions on a worldview. A person may not be able to identify his worldview, and it may lack consistency, but his most basic assumptions about the origin of life, purpose, and the future guarantee adherence to some system of thought.[1]

That definition may do nothing more for you than make you yawn, but you need to know that this is HUGE. Your worldview really does matter, and it really does affect the way you think and act.

Look at it this way: Each day, you have a limitless

number of options, which are all affected by your worldview:

1. Moral decisions
2. Political views
3. Social options
4. Scientific views
5. College selection
6. Career paths
7. Choices of friends
8. Artistic preferences
9. Financial decisions
10. Time management
11. Leisure activities

How do you decide what to do? What is your guiding principle? What is it that's turning your rudder in the right direction and telling your conscience to do the right thing? It's your worldview. That is what's guiding you in your choices, whether you know it or not.

A person's worldview is evident by what one does with his or her life. Life is a sacred trust, and choices must be made in relation to proper purposes, which require a worldview.
DR. PAUL COX

You Have Two Choices

It's not an oversimplification to say that you only have two worldview choices. Your worldview either includes God or it doesn't. Here are two handy checklists.

A Worldview Without God

- God is not in the picture.
- All things in the world, including humanity, evolved by naturalistic means, without any supernatural input.
- As the highest evolved species, humanity is the measure of all things and the ultimate authority.
- There is no absolute truth; personal choice is what's most important.
- The government is the highest law, and government can and must decide what's best for people in areas ranging from business to moral behavior.

A Worldview with God

- God is the creator of and the supreme being in the universe.

- God created all things, including human beings.
- Because humans are created in the image of God, we all have dignity and purpose.
- God's revealed absolute truth comes first; we build our personal beliefs and choices around it.
- God has ordained government as a means of keeping order in an imperfect world.

The Big Lie

You're going to hear the "everyone goes to heaven" argument more than you'll hear the "God doesn't exist" argument. It's very fashionable in today's culture for people to talk about spiritual things. They'll even talk about God—but not the living, personal God who is involved in history and, more specifically, in your life. To them, God is more of a concept or an idea that wouldn't exist if humanity hadn't invented Him. In fact, many people believe that they are God and God is them.

This is what we call the Big Lie, and it's nothing new. Satan used this argument in the Garden of Eden when he told Adam and Eve, "You will become just like God, knowing everything, both good and evil" (Genesis 3:5).

Adam and Eve bought into the Big Lie. But rather than becoming just like God, they became enemies of God—and so did the rest of the human race (which is why nothing has changed today). The Big Lie didn't die with Adam and Eve. You are likely to come across people who give the same message in books and on talk shows: You are God. What these misguided individuals are saying may be clever and appealing, but it's still the Big Lie.

True Truth

But you know better than that, don't you? You know that in order for something to be true, it must be true for everyone. Truth is not something that's true for you but not for everyone else. The common argument you will hear today is that, even though people have different ideas about truth, it's okay, as long as they agree to disagree.

We're not talking about opinions, such as, "I thought the movie was good." That's not truth—it's an opinion—because someone else may not like the movie. Truth goes something like, "If I jump off this 10-story building, I'm going to really hurt myself and probably die." No one can say, "Well, that's your opinion." It's truth for everyone.

When it comes to God, you must operate in the area of truth, not opinion. Better yet, you need to think about *true* truth, because God is the ultimate source of truth. There will always be other voices—your college professors, the media, your friends, some mystic writer, a guest on *Oprah*—who will say they have the truth. It will be your job to sort out the voices, which is no easy task. But you must do it, and you must get good at it, for one simple reason: *Your life depends on it!*

Faith Matters

Wouldn't it be great if you could put God under a microscope or view Him through a telescope and actually *see* Him with your own eyes? Then you could say, "Look, there He is. There's God. Now I believe!"

The truth is, people have seen the *evidence* for God under the microscope and through the telescope. The incredible order and design of the universe—from the tiniest molecule to the most distant stars—point to the existence of a personal, intelligent, loving designer. The Bible puts it this way:

> From the time the world was created, people have seen the earth and sky and all that God made. They can clearly see his invisible qualities—his eternal power and divine nature. So they have no excuse whatsoever for not knowing God (Romans 1:20).

Still, none of us has actually ever *seen* God, which means that ultimately you have to have *faith* to believe the evidence about God, which comes through nature, through your heart, through the Bible and ultimately through Jesus Christ.

> What is faith? It is the confident assurances that what we hope for is going to happen. It is the evidence of things we cannot yet see. (Hebrews 11:1)

Faith, which is the same as trust, is what ultimately matters. Faith in God through Jesus Christ is what counts. But it isn't a blind faith. It's faith based on evidence.

Be Ready to Give an Answer

As you get out in the world, whether that's college or a job or just living on your own, your beliefs are going to be challenged by the skepticism and the lifestyles of just about everyone around you. In your classes and in your work, you will probably encounter indifference—if not hostility—toward belief in the one true God (that's why it's so important to surround yourself with Christian friends).

That's okay. Don't be discouraged. God has you there for a reason, and that reason is to represent and glorify Him. And don't be offended. Many people in the world are hostile to the things of God. The apostle Paul, a brilliant thinker and debater, received this hostility personally after preaching the truth about God. He wrote, "I know how foolish the message of the cross sounds to those who are on the road to destruction. But we who are being saved recognize this message as the very power of God" (1 Corinthians 1:18).

You've probably heard the expression that the best offense is a great defense. When it comes to the things of God, that is true. You don't need to go on the offensive to attack those who don't believe. Simply study the Bible diligently, and be ready to give an answer when someone asks you about your faith (see 2 Timothy 2:15; 1 Peter 3:15-17).

The Value of Christian Friendship

It's one thing to study the truth about God on your own and quite another to find other people who are doing the same thing. You need to fellowship with (which means to communicate with) other believers who can encourage you and pray for you (and you for them).

If you are planning to attend a Christian college, it's going to be easy for you to find people who believe the things you believe. If you're planning to attend a secular college or university, or if you're joining the workforce, then it's going to take a little effort to find other Christians. Fortunately, you can find at least one of several outstanding Christian ministries on most college campuses. We recommend these:

- Campus Crusade for Christ (www.ccci.org)
- InterVarsity Christian Fellowship (www.intervarsity.org)
- Collegiate Navigators (www.gospelcom.net/navs/collegiate)

For information on Catholic churches and ministries near you, check out RCNet (www.rc.net).

In addition to the fellowship these campus ministries can provide, it is absolutely essential that you find a local church. Even if you have had a negative experience at a church in the past, you need to give going to church another chance. Realize that the Church isn't a building or a program. The Church is you and all believers. The Bible says that Christ loved the Church and "gave up his life for her" (Ephesians 5:25).

Seek This First

Having a worldview that includes God has tremendous implications, not just for your future, but also for your life right now. You don't just live with that worldview when you go to church or when you're around other Christians. It's something that is a part of you every single minute of your life. Sure, you have questions and concerns and worries about what you're going to do both now and in the future. That's normal. But you can't let them dominate your life and hinder your relationship with God. You need to trust that God loves you and cares for you in every detail of your life.

Moving On

In this chapter, we've asked you to consider what your life would be like without God and why you're so much better off with God in your worldview and your life. You could say that we've given you the *macro*view of God.

In the next chapter—yes, the *last* chapter—we're going to look at the *micro*view of God (no, that doesn't mean God is a tiny speck). What we mean is that we're going to look at what it takes to have a daily, practical and very real relationship with God. These are the details of your life that you can't just push aside—not if you want your life to be as exciting and effective as it can possibly be.

Those Things You Do

What God Wants for You

After high school, you'll know whether you went to church because your parents made you or because you had a strong faith. Stay strong in what you believe. It's hard when your relationship with God is lacking. Nothing is worse.

HOLLY S., AGE 21

God is a perfect gentleman. He is always available to you, but He won't intrude on you. He waits for you to seek Him. That means, of course, that you are going to have to find time for God in the midst of all of your activities. It won't be easy, because there will be many things competing for your time: friends, college, job and, occasionally, sleep.

In the last chapter we talked about how God deserves to have top priority in our lives. In this chapter we'll talk about practical ways that you can make sure that will happen.

Lose Your Parents' Faith

Does the heading to this section shock you? (If you aren't shocked, at least your parents will be.) Let us explain what we mean. For about 18 years you have been living under your parents' roof and have been abiding (more or less) by their rules. You have adhered to their principles and respected their opinions. Much of what they believe has probably rubbed off on you. You might have even adopted their faith as your own without many questions.

Having your parents' faith may have gotten you through high school, but it won't cut it in the real world after high school. Your beliefs are going to be questioned, challenged and attacked. If you don't know what you believe and why you believe it, your faith will be crushed.

We aren't saying that you can't have the same faith in God that your parents have. But you need to understand that it has to be *your* faith. Your relationship with God needs to be personal—you and Him. You cannot have a relationship with God vicariously (through your parents).

> **You won't get to heaven just because your parents have faith in Jesus. God doesn't have any grandchildren.**

Stay Connected to God

Suppose that a few years from now you fall in love and become engaged to be married. How would you feel if, during the period of your engagement, you never received a call or a visit from your future spouse? Oh, there were good intentions to spend time with you, but too many activities got in the way. Well, we all know that your wedding plans would be tossed in the dumpster.

Imagine how God feels when we ignore Him. We might have good intentions, but they frequently fizzle out. Do we really expect to wake up at 5 A.M. for a little Bible reading if we were at a party until after midnight? Fortunately, God won't throw us in the dumpster, but we can't expect that our relationship with Him will develop if we are continually giving Him just the leftovers of our time and energy.

Talking to God

Prayer is nothing more than talking to God. We don't mean that it is an insignificant endeavor—quite the contrary. Talking one-on-one with the Creator of the universe is a huge deal. But many people get all flustered by it because they think they have to talk to God in a strange, uncomfortable way.

- *They may think they have to use old-fashioned English phrases.* They throw in a lot of "thee" and "thou" expressions. Basically, they must think that God likes to hear people talk like Shakespeare.
- *They may think they must make their voice sound "spiritual."* All that happens is that they end up sounding like the narrator at the Haunted Mansion in Disneyland. (God isn't scared by

it, but we don't think that He wants us to feel obligated to get voice lessons in order to talk to Him.)

- *They may think they must engage in some long and protracted soliloquy that reviews the history of mankind and covers all people—living and dead—who have ever populated the globe (and who must be mentioned by name).* If this is your understanding of prayer, then you can only do it if you can spare an entire evening and can talk for several hours without breathing.

Prayer should be like natural conversation: Talk to God about what is bugging you; thank Him for how He has taken care of you; ask Him for guidance in the problem areas of your life.

Just be yourself when you are talking to God, but remember who He is.

- *Don't treat God like some sort of celestial vending machine* that will drop whatever you want down from heaven.
- *Don't patronize Him.* He is not some old, senile, drooling grandfather in the sky. He is not going to fall for your "If I do this for you, then you should do this for me" routine.

- *Be honest with Him.* After all, He knows when you are being truthful and when you are being hypocritical, so don't try to fake it with Him.

The important thing about prayer is that you do it regularly.

Why Do I Need to Say Anything to a Mind Reader?

You're probably wondering, *Since God knows everything, including what I'm going to say, then why should I pray to Him?* That's a fair question. We think that prayer is for our benefit—yours and ours—not God's. When you pray,

- you remind yourself that God is in control;
- you acknowledge that He deserves your worship; and
- you curb your pride and independence by submitting your concerns to Him.

Listening to God

There are two ways that you listen to God. The first is by being quiet during some of your prayer time. You can't hear God speak to you in your thoughts if you are doing all of the talking.

The other way to hear what God says is to read the Bible. After all, the Bible contains His words, and it was written for you. We know that Bible reading can seem like a chore at times, but that is usually because people have the wrong attitude about it.

- They may think the Bible is an antiquated history book with no relevance for today.
- They may think the Bible is full of a bunch of fairy tales and has no relevance for real life.
- They may be intimidated by the size of the book—lots of pages, fine print and no pictures (though sometimes some nifty maps).
- They may fall asleep while reading it (which usually happens because they are reading at the end of the day when they are in their pajamas and tucked under the covers).

On the other hand, you will find great excitement in the Bible when you remember that it is

- the owner's manual for your life, which has been painstakingly written by your manufacturer;
- a true, historical account of intergalactic battles between the forces of good and evil (and

you are the prize that they are fighting over);
- a manual for success in the areas of relationships, finance and employment; and
- a guide for the future—your future—that will
tell you precisely how your world is going to
end and what happens after that.

The important thing about studying the Bible
(just like prayer) is that you do it regularly.

Check Out the Body

The New Testament describes the Church as the "body
of Christ" (1 Corinthians 12:12) and compares each
follower of Christ to a body part. This analogy tells
you two things (to illustrate them, we will assume that
you are the large intestine in this body):

- First, the Church won't work properly if you
aren't participating. A body needs its large
intestine to function properly.
- Second, you won't be spiritually functioning
as God designed if you aren't participating in
a church. You will be just like a large intestine
flopping around all by itself, unconnected to
the rest of the body. What a mess.

When you are out on your own, you'll be tempted to skip church from time to time. Don't do it. Get connected with a group of believers so that you are encouraged and held accountable in your spiritual walk.

Which Church Is the Right One?

If you move away from home, you will be faced with the task of finding a church in your new town. There will probably be a lot of churches to choose from. How do you know which one is right for you? Good question.

Here are a few clues for finding a good church:

- *Start by looking for a church that's similar to the one you attended at home.* Remember that there may be some tough going in your new circumstances and you may need a place where you feel spiritually "at home."
- *Look for a church that focuses on the Bible.* Does the minister preach from the Bible? Is he interested in the words of God, or is he preaching sermons like "The Importance of a Smile" and "Do Your Part to Prevent Forest Fires"?
- *Seek a church with a family atmosphere.* Are you going to be able to meet and know people at a

meaningful level? Your church experience needs to be more than just sitting through a praise chorus concert (although that type of worship is great); you need to be developing deep friendships with other believers.

- *If transportation is a problem, search for a church that has a ministry for college students on your campus.* The chances are good that arrangements for transportation are available. There may be churches that offer Bible studies and other activities on campus.

- *Look for a church that offers service opportunities.* As a college student, your life will be lived in a bit of a bubble. In many respects it can be extremely easy for college students to isolate themselves from the rest of the world. You may be interested in finding a church that gives you opportunity to serve, both at the church and in the community.

An important part about going to church is that you do it regularly. This doesn't win you extra credit with God, but it will help you personally, and your participation will help the other members in your church family.

How Can I Find Christ on Campus?

As we discussed in chapter 2, you will have some interesting challenges if you are attending a secular college or university. If that is the case, then find a Christian group on campus. There are many organizations designed for Christian college students—Campus Crusade, Collegiate Navigators and InterVarsity, among others (their websites are listed in chapter 11). While these groups don't replace your need to be involved in a church, they are designed to provide you with a Christian support group on campus and in the dorms.

How Can I Know God's Will?

As we spend time talking about issues of the Christian faith with people your age, there is one question that keeps popping up: How can I know God's will for my life? That is a great question, and you'd probably like to know the answer to it.

Well, we'd like to give you a definitive answer to it, but we don't have one. We are convinced that there is no single formula for finding God's will, but there are some principles that might be helpful to you in the process of seeking His direction for your life.

Seven Things That We're Learning About God's Will

1. *God isn't trying to play a guessing game with you.* He is not trying to make His will difficult to find. He is anxious for you to know what He desires for you.

2. *Most of the time, there is not one single, overriding plan for your life.* Don't worry that you might guess wrong and get stuck with God's Plan B for your life instead of the better Plan A. Some people fret that if they make one minor misjudgment of God's will, then they will be off track for the rest of their lives. (For example, you might worry, *Oh, what if I should have taken the World Civ course instead of Psychology? What if the person God wanted me to marry was in the World Civ class? Now I will never meet that person, and I'll get stuck marrying somebody else.*) Think about it. Before the world was created, God knew what choices you would make. He is not going to be surprised by what you choose, and He can work the circumstances around your choices.

3. *There are a lot of areas where God's will doesn't matter.* For example, we don't think He particularly cares which breakfast cereal you choose or which parking space you select.

4. *God's will has momentum.* It seems that He moves us

along in the direction that we are supposed to be going. Drastic changes at the spur of the moment are possible in God's will, but it seems that He usually goes with a more methodical approach. (For example, before He calls you to be a missionary in China, He might have you working in a cross-cultural ministry in your hometown.)

5. *God equips you for doing His will.* He has given you a specific personality and spiritual gifts. He has given you certain aptitudes, talents and skills. Don't you think it is likely that His will for your life is going to involve your unique characteristics?

6. *Prayer plays a big part in knowing God's will.* Remember that prayer involves listening to God as much as it does talking to Him. Don't expect to hear a James Earl Jones-type voice booming down from heaven. Instead, allow God to direct your thoughts in the quietness of your prayer time with Him.

7. *God's will isn't so much a time or a place or a person. It is primarily a condition of your heart.* God wants you to be willing to serve and follow Him. He wants you to be moldable and moveable. You should spend your time working on your relationship with Him, and let Him be responsible for arranging the circumstances of your life to guide you where He wants you to be.

Here's an amazing thought: Everything you need to know about God's will is in the Bible. Now, don't panic. It is not revealed in some secret, obscure verse in Habakkuk that you have never read (although there may be quite a few verses in Habakkuk that you've never read). Nope. It is right there in plain view in the New Testament.

> Jesus replied, "'You must love the Lord your God with all your heart, all your soul, and all your mind.' This is the first and greatest commandment. A second is equally important: 'Love your neighbor as yourself'" (Matthew 22:37-39).

There it is! That's God's will for you—that you love Him and show love to those around you.

We can almost hear you thinking, *It can't be as simple as that!* But it is. If you are actively involved in knowing and loving God and if you are obeying Him, then you are doing His will for your life.

Moving On

In this book, whenever you came to the Moving On section, we sent you to the next chapter—until now.

Now it really is time for you to move on—past the back cover of this book and into real life.

We are sincerely excited about what lies ahead for you in your life after high school. Yes, there will be a mix of thrills and tragedies, but we are confident that you are going to find adventure in all of the experiences that are part of your new responsibilities and freedom.

We like the way Peter ended his first epistle to the Christians in Asia Minor:

> My purpose in writing is to encourage you and assure you that the grace of God is with you no matter what happens (1 Peter 5:12).

That is our purpose in writing this book to you. We hope you have been encouraged to step boldly into life after high school with the realization that God wants to lead you in that journey.

Endnotes

Chapter 5

1. Alan Loy McGinnis, *The Friendship Factor* (Minneapolis, MN: Augsburg Publishing House, 1979), p. 22.

Chapter 8

1. "New Surgeon General's Report Expands List of Diseases Caused by Smoking," *United States Department of Health and Human Services,* May 27, 2004. http://www.hhs.gov/news/press/2004pres/20040527a.html (accessed January 6, 2005).

2. L. D. Johnston, et al., "Cigarette Smoking Among American Teens Continues to Decline, but More Slowly Than in the Past" (Ann Arbor, MI: University of Michigan News and Information Services, 2004). http://www.monitoringthefuture.org/data/04data.html#2004data-cigs (accessed January 6, 2005).

3. Ibid.

4. Christopher D. Hudson, et al., *College Clues for the Clueless* (Uhrichsville, Ohio: Promise Press, 1999), p. 198.

5. Cheryl Townsley, *Food Smart!* (New York: Jeremy P. Tarcher/Putman, 1997), p. 92.

6. Stormie Omartian, *Greater Health God's Way* (Eugene, OR: Harvest House Publishers, 1996), p. 138.

Chapter 10

1. UNESCO Institute for Statistics, "Adult Illiteracy Rate and Population by Gender," adult illiteracy chart, July 2002. http://www.uis.unesco.org/en/stats/statistics/literacy2000.htm (accessed January 6, 2005).

Chapter 11

1. David Noebel, *Understanding the Times* (Eugene, OR: Harvest House Publishers, 1991), p. 1.

Bibliography

Bickel, Bruce, and Jantz, Stan. *Bible Prophecy 101.* Eugene, OR: Harvest House Publishers, 2004.

——. *Knowing God 101.* Eugene, OR: Harvest House Publishers, 2004.

Biehl, Bobb. *Mentoring: Confidence in Finding a Mentor and Becoming One.* Nashville, TN: Broadman and Holman, 1997.

Covey, Stephen R. *The Seven Habits of Highly Effective People.* New York: Simon and Schuster, 1989.

Dobson, James. *Life on the Edge.* Nashville, TN: Word Publishing, 1995.

Gimbel, James R., ed. *The Campus Connection.* St. Louis, MO: Concordia Publishing House, 1998.

Harris, Joshua. *I Kissed Dating Goodbye.* Sisters, OR: Multnomah Books, 1997.

Hudsen, Christopher D., et al. *College Clues for the Clueless.* Uhrichsville, OH: Promise Press, 1999.

Kallgren, Robert C., and Beyer, Byran E. "Bible Breath: Too Much?" in *Today's Guide to Christian Colleges.* Barrington, IL: Real Media Group, 1999.

McDowell, Josh, and Wilson, Bill. *A Ready Defense.* Nashville, TN: Thomas Nelson Publishers, 1993.

McGinnis, Alan Loy. *The Friendship Factor.* Minneapolis,

MN: Augsburg Publishing House, 1979.

Noebel, David. *Understanding the Times*. Eugene, OR: Harvest House Publishers, 1991.

Omartian, Stormie. *Greater Health God's Way*. Eugene, OR: Harvest House Publishers, 1996.

Smith, Michael W. *It's Time to Be Bold*. Nashville, TN: Word Publishers, 1997.

Townsley, Cheryl. *Food Smart!* New York: Jeremy P. Tarcher/Putnam, 1997.

Warren, Neil Clark. *Finding the Love of Your Life*. Wheaton, IL: Tyndale House Publishers, 1992.

Worthington, Janet Farrar, and Farrar, Ronald. *The Ultimate College Survival Guide*. Princeton, NJ: Peterson's, 1998.

More Outstanding Resources for Students from Regal

Addicted to God
50 Days to a More
Powerful Relationship
with God
Jim Burns
ISBN 08307.25318

No Compromise
A Passionate Devotional
to Ignite Your Faith
Jim Burns
ISBN 08307.29127

Letters from Home
Everything You Need
to Know to Be
Successful in Life
Ted Haggard
ISBN 08307.30583

Free
A 40-Day Devotional
Connecting with Jesus, the
Source of True Freedom
Neil T. Anderson
and *Dave Park*
ISBN 08307.36964

**Stomping Out
Depression**
Overcoming Depression
Neil T. Anderson
and *Dave Park*
ISBN 08307.28929

**Stomping Out
the Darkness**
Find Out Who You Are in
Christ and Why You Don't
Have to Put Up with the
World's Garbage Anymore!
Neil T. Anderson
and *Dave Park*
ISBN 08307.32888

Pick Up a Copy at Your Favorite Christian Bookstore!

Visit **www.regalbooks.com** to join **Regal's FREE e-newsletter.**
You'll get useful **excerpts from our newest releases** and **special
access to online chats with your favorite authors.** Sign up today!

Regal
God's Word for Your World™
www.regalbooks.com

**Saving My
First Kiss**
Why I'm Keeping
Confetti in My Closet
Lisa Velthouse
ISBN 08307.34872

**Prayers for When
You're Mad, Sad
or Just Totally
Confused**
Brittany Waggoner
ISBN 08307.34724

Soul Sister
The Truth About
Being God's Girl
Beth Redman
ISBN 08307.32128

True Beauty
The Inside Story
Devotions for You
and Your Friends
Andrea Stephens
ISBN 08307.35097

**Stuff a Girl's
Gotta Know**
Little Hints for Big Things
in a Teen's Life
Andrea Stephens
ISBN 08307.34996

Pick Up a Copy at Your Favorite Christian Bookstore!

Visit **www.regalbooks.com** to join **Regal's FREE e-newsletter.**
You'll get useful **excerpts from our newest releases** and **special
access to online chats with your favorite authors.** Sign up today!

God's Word for Your World™
www.regalbooks.com